# Increase of Revelation and Restoration: Reveal, Recover & Restore

Bill Vincent

Published by RWG Publishing, 2021.

While every precaution has been taken in the preparation of this book, the publisher assumes no responsibility for errors or omissions, or for damages resulting from the use of the information contained herein.

INCREASE OF REVELATION AND RESTORATION: REVEAL, RECOVER & RESTORE

**First edition. July 30, 2021.**

Copyright © 2021 Bill Vincent.

Written by Bill Vincent.

# Also by Bill Vincent

Building a Prototype Church: Divine Strategies Released
Experience God's Love: By Revival Waves of Glory School of the Supernatural
Glory: Expanding God's Presence
Glory: Increasing God's Presence
Glory: Kingdom Presence of God
Glory: Pursuing God's Presence
Glory: Revival Presence of God
Rapture Revelations: Jesus Is Coming
The Prototype Church: Heaven's Strategies for Today's Church
The Secret Place of God's Power
Transitioning Into a Prototype Church: New Church Arising
Spiritual Warfare Made Simple
Aligning With God's Promises
A Closer Relationship With God
Armed for Battle: Spiritual Warfare Battle Commands
Breakthrough of Spiritual Strongholds
Desperate for God's Presence: Understanding Supernatural Atmospheres
Destroying the Jezebel Spirit: How to Overcome the Spirit Before It Destroys You!
Discerning Your Call of God

Glory: Expanding God's Presence: Discover How to Manifest God's Glory

Glory: Kingdom Presence Of God: Secrets to Becoming Ambassadors of Christ

Satan's Open Doors: Access Denied

Spiritual Warfare: The Complete Collection

The War for Spiritual Battles: Identify Satan's Strategies

Understanding Heaven's Court System: Explosive Life Changing Secrets

A Godly Shaking: Don't Create Waves

Faith: A Connection of God's Power

Global Warning: Prophetic Details Revealed

Overcoming Obstacles

Spiritual Leadership: Kingdom Foundation Principles

Glory: Revival Presence of God: Discover How to Release Revival Glory

Increasing Your Prophetic Gift: Developing a Pure Prophetic Flow

Millions of Churches: Why Is the World Going to Hell?

The Supernatural Realm: Discover Heaven's Secrets

The Unsearchable Riches of Christ: Chosen to be Sons of God

Deep Hunger: God Will Change Your Appetite Toward Him

Defeating the Demonic Realm

Glory: Increasing God's Presence: Discover New Waves of God's Glory

Growing In the Prophetic: Developing a Prophetic Voice

Healing After Divorce: Grace, Mercy and Remarriage

Love is Waiting

Awakening of Miracles: Personal Testimonies of God's Healing Power

Deception and Consequences Revealed: You Shall Know the Truth and the Truth Shall Set You Free

Overcoming the Power of Lust

Are You a Follower of Christ: Discover True Salvation

Cover Up and Save Yourself: Revealing Sexy is Not Sexy

Heaven's Court System: Bringing Justice for All

The Angry Fighter's Story: Harness the Fire Within

The Wrestler: The Pursuit of a Dream

Beginning the Courts of Heaven: Understanding the Basics

Breaking Curses: Legal Rights in the Courts of Heaven

Writing and Publishing a Book: Secrets of a Christian Author

How to Write a Book: Step by Step Guide

The Anointing: Fresh Oil of God's Presence

Spiritual Leadership: Kingdom Foundation Principles Second Edition

The Courts of Heaven: How to Present Your Case

The Jezebel Spirit: Tactics of Jezebel's Control

Heaven's Angels: The Nature and Ranking of Angels

Don't Know What to Do?: Discover Promotion in the Wilderness

Word of the Lord: Prophetic Word for 2020

The Coronavirus Prophecy

Increase Your Anointing: Discover the Supernatural

Apostolic Breakthrough: Birthing God's Purposes

The Healing Power of God: Releasing the Power of the Holy Spirit

The Secret Place of God's Power: Revelations of God's Word

The Rapture: Details of the Second Coming of Christ

Increase of Revelation and Restoration: Reveal, Recover & Restore

Restoration of the Soul: The Presence of God Changes Everything
Building a Prototype Church: The Church is in a Season of Profound of Change
Keys to Receiving Your Miracle: Miracles Happen Today
The Resurrection Power of God: Great Exploits of God
Transitioning to the Prototype Church: The Church is in a Season of Profound of Transition
Waves of Revival: Expect the Unexpected
The Stronghold of Jezebel: A True Story of a Man's Journey
Glory: Pursuing God's Presence: Revealing Secrets
Like a Mighty Rushing Wind
Steps to Revival
Supernatural Power
The Goodness of God
The Secret to Spiritual Strength
The Glorious Church's Birth: Understanding God's Plan For Our Lives
God's Presence Has a Profound Impact On Us
Spiritual Battles of the Mind: When All Hell Breaks Loose, Heaven Sends Help
A Godly Shaking Coming to the Church: Churches are Being Rerouted
Relationship with God in a New Way
The Spirit of God's Anointing: Using the Holy Spirit's Power in You
The Magnificent Church: God's Power Is Being Manifested
Miracles Are Awakened: Today is a Day of Miracles
Prepared to Fight: The Battle of Deliverance
The Journey of a Faithful: Adhering to the teachings of Jesus Christ

Ascension to the Top of Spiritual Mountains: Putting an End to Pain Cycles

After Divorce Recovery: When I Think of Grace, I Think of Mercy and Remarriage

A Greater Sense of God's Presence: Learn How to Make God's Glory Visible

Do Not Allow the Enemy to Steal: To a Crown of Righteousness, a Crown of Thorns

There Are Countless Churches: What is the Cause of Global Doom?

Creating a Model Church: The Church is Undergoing Considerable Upheaval

Developing Your Prophetic Ability: Creating a Flow of Pure Prophetic Intent

Christ's Limitless Riches Are Unsearchable: God Has Chosen Us to Be His Sons

Faith is a Link Between God's Might and Ours

Increasing the Presence of God: The Revival of the End-Times Is Approaching

Getting a Prophecy for Yourself: Unlocking Your Prophecies with Prophetic Keys

Getting Rid of the Jezebel Spirit: Before the Spirit Destroys You, Here's How to Overcome It!

Getting to Know Heaven's Court System: Secrets That Will Change Your Life

God's Resurrected Presence: Revival Glory is Being Released

God's Presence In His Kingdom: Secrets to Becoming Christ's Ambassadors

God's Healing Ability: The Holy Spirit's Power is Being Released

God's Power of Resurrection: God's Great Exploits

Heaven's Supreme Court: Providing Equal Justice for All
Increasing God's Presence in Our Lives: God's Glory Has Reached New Heights
Jezebel's Stronghold: This is the Story of an Actual Man's Journey
Making the Shift to the Model Church: The Church Is In the Midst of a Major Shift
Overcoming Lust's Influence: The Way to Victory
Pursuing God's Presence: Disclosing Information
The Plan to Take Over America: Restoring, We the People and the Power of God
Revelation and Restoration Are Increasing: The Process That Reveals, Recovers, and Restores
Burn In the Presence of the Lord
Revival Tidal Waves: Be Prepared for the Unexpected
Taking down the Demonic Realm: Curses and Revelations of Demonic Spirits
The Apocalypse: Details about Christ's Second Coming
The Hidden Resource of God's Power
The Open Doors of Satan: Access is Restricted
The Secrets to Getting Your Miracle
The Truth About Deception and Its Consequences
The Universal World: Discover the Mysteries of Heaven
Warning to the World: Details of Prophecies Have Been Revealed
Wonders and Significance: God's Glory in New Waves
Word of the Lord
Why Is There No Lasting Revival: It's Time For the Next Move of God
A Double New Beginning: A Prophetic Word, the Best Is Yet to Come

Your Most Productive Season Ever: The Anointing to Get Things Done
Break Free From Prison: No More Bondage for the Saints
Breaking Strongholds: Taking Steps to Freedom
Carrying the Glory of God: Igniting the End Time Revival
Breakthrough Over the Enemies Attack on Resources: An Angel Called Breakthrough
Days of Breakthrough: Your Time is Now
Empowered For the Unprecedented: Extraordinary Days Ahead
The Ultimate Guide to Self-Publishing: How to Write, Publish, and Promote Your Book for Free
The Art of Writing: A Comprehensive Guide to Crafting Your Masterpiece
The Non-Fiction Writer's Guide: Mastering Engaging Narratives
Spiritual Leadership (Large Print Edition): Kingdom Foundation Principles
Desperate for God's Presence (Large Print Edition): Understanding Supernatural Atmospheres
From Writer to Marketer: How to Successfully Promote Your Self-Published Book
Unleashing Your Inner Author: A Step-by-Step Guide to Crafting Your Own Bestseller
Becoming a YouTube Sensation: A Guide to Success
The Art of Content Creation: Tips and Tricks for YouTube
Signs and Wonders Revelations: Experience Heaven on Earth

Watch for more at
https://revivalwavesofgloryministries.com/.

# Introduction

You are about to discover some of what the entire Church needs to receive. This book will start out with discovering all that God has granted for us to know.

The enemy has stolen and robbed so many for centuries. It is time to learn how we are to recover and see full restoration. God wants to stir restoration to such a level that it will release a restoration movement where all that has been lost or stolen will be restored. You will receive much revelation through this breakthrough book.

# It Has Been Established

God has determined and is determining whom He shall release increase in this hour. A Revival was foretold and orchestrated by the Holy Spirit through an angelic visitation highlighting many Cities in which the Spirit of restoration would bring to this generation seeds of power and revival released.

Look very closely at this scripture released in the midst of revival, Isaiah 6:9, 10 And he said, Go, and tell this people, Hear ye indeed, but understand not; and see ye indeed, but perceive not. Make the heart of this people fat, and make their ears heavy, and shut their eyes; lest they see with their eyes, and hear with their ears, and understand with their heart, and convert, and be healed. The anointing has been so strong; I don't believe people initially recognized the content of the word that is being expressed. Who would want a prophetic word declaring their eyes to be dim and their ears dull unless they should see and hear the day of their visitation and return to the Lord and be healed.

Matthew 13:11-16 He answered and said unto them, Because it is given unto you to know the mysteries of the kingdom of heaven, but to them it is not given. For whosoever hath, to him shall be given, and he shall have more abundance: but whosoever hath not, from him shall be taken away even that he hath. Therefore speak I to them in parables: because they seeing see not; and hearing they hear not, neither do they understand. And in them is fulfilled the prophecy of Esaias, which saith, By hearing ye shall hear, and shall not understand; and seeing ye shall see, and shall not perceive: For this people's heart is waxed gross, and *their* ears are dull of hearing, and their eyes they have closed; lest at any time they should see with *their* eyes, and hear with *their* ears, and should understand with *their* heart, and should be converted, and I should heal them. But blessed *are* your eyes, for they see: and your ears, for they hear.

The Holy Spirit has come upon us to provide an incredible confirmation of the message the Lord desires to establish within us during this decisive hour of purpose and destiny...TO US IT HAS BEEN GRANTED TO KNOW THE MYSTERIES OF THE KINGDOM.

Isaiah 6 clearly prophesies the Spirit of Revelation that is necessary to illumine our eyes and ears, was withheld from that generation of people in order that they could not recognize the day of their visitation.

The scriptures point out, if they had then they would have surely returned to the Lord and He would be required, according to His promise, to heal them.

Thankfully, we have the biblical pledge that we do not have to remain in such a condition. Although Isaiah rightly prophesied concerning a generation whose ears were dull and whose eyes were dim and unable to recognize the day of their visitation, we have the revelatory assurance that...To us it has been granted to know the mysteries of the kingdom.

It is our right, privilege and admonition to be anointed with the Spirit of revelation that our eyes would be illumined and our ears unstopped that we might know and understand the mysteries of the kingdom. In other words, we have the right to be anointed with the Spirit of revelation which brings insight to us concerning the mind, will and purpose of God in the earth and the unveiling of His Kingdom.

One of the things most adamantly opposed by the enemy is the full release of this Spirit upon the church. Our adversary knows that if God's people are anointed with the prophetic mandate to be clothed with revelation, then we would return to the Lord and He would have to heal us. That healing would not merely consist of physical and emotional restoration, but also fully mending the breach that has existed between God and man since the Garden of Eden. Once accomplished, the reality of "CHRIST IN US-—THE HOPE OF GLORY" becomes apparent and we walk in the prophetic destiny foretold in the scriptures. That is the reason there has been so much opposition to the emerging prophetic generation.

Ephesians 1:17, 18 That the God of our Lord Jesus Christ, the Father of glory, may give unto you the spirit of wisdom and revelation in the knowledge of him: The eyes of your understanding being enlightened; that ye may know what is the hope of his calling, and what the riches of the glory of his inheritance in the saints,

This form of wisdom is not merely the ability to mentally analyze a situation and make a good response. Rather, it is a spiritual endowment that allows us to go deep into the heart of the Father to see and understand the mysteries of the kingdom and our rights through redemption. Not only do we have the right to understand these mysteries but also the right to the accompanying Spirit of revelation which gives illumination and comprehension of their reality.

Ephesians 1:17-19 That the God of our Lord Jesus Christ, the Father of glory, may give unto you the spirit of wisdom and revelation in the knowledge of him: The eyes of your understanding being enlightened; that ye may know what is the hope of his calling, and what the riches of the glory of his inheritance in the saints, And what *is* the exceeding greatness of his power to us-ward who believe, according to the working of his mighty power,

The spirit of wisdom is more clearly defined as a supernatural impartation of the Spirit granting the ability to see and recognize the Lord Jesus with a spiritual knowledge and comprehension of His mysteries, plans and purposes. This heritage will reveal the manifold and unsearchable wisdom and secrets of God that are hidden in Christ. It relates to a deeper intimacy and awareness into the things of God and intimates a personal close encounter with the Lord. The accompanying spirit of revelation grants a comprehension of these mysteries and attributes of God. It involves an understanding and perception with our soul of these things revealed in the spirit. It grants us the ability to not only know the things of God but also the practical application of them in the earth and in our lives.

The Apostle Paul was anointed and flowed with this Spirit as he continually conveyed the mysteries of the Kingdom to his generation. This same Spirit is essential for us in this generation to know the concealed secrets reserved for the last days and share in the hidden manna set aside for the end-time perfecting of the Bride.

# INCREASE OF REVELATION AND RESTORATION: REVEAL, RECOVER & RESTORE

Daniel 12:4 But thou, O Daniel, shut up the words, and seal the book, *even* to the time of the end: many shall run to and fro, and knowledge shall be increased.

According to Ephesians 1:18-19; it provides three blessings essential for our ability to walk in the full measure of Christ through the eyes of our heart being enlightened.

(1) That we may know what is the Hope of His Calling

(2) What are the riches of the glory of His inheritance in the Saints?

(3) What is the surpassing greatness of His power toward us who believe?

When we read these words our minds recognize the great promise that has been provided to us. Even so, when anointed with the spirit of wisdom and revelation, we begin to obtain a comprehension experientially of the reality of this redemptive birthright.

As the scriptures point out, eye has not seen, ear has not heard nor has it entered into the heart of man all the great blessings the Lord has provided for us. These must be revealed by the Spirit.

To us it has been granted and to fully apprehend this exceptional mystery. To us it has been granted in this generation to be anointed with the Spirit of revelation to know and comprehend these great mysteries provided for us through the awesome power of redemption. One of the greatest mysteries that will be fully realized is the wonder of Christ in us the Hope of Glory.

We recite the words but very few experientially discover the absolute and complete reality. However, we believe the scriptures have promised that an entire company of believers will soon emerge anointed with this certainty, walking in the fullness of it with great power and authority and, more importantly, radiating the nature and character of Christ through His manifested Glory.

It is especially noteworthy that the full revelation required the joining together of the minstrel and prophetic mantel. This in itself depicts the emerging partnership between worship and the prophetic, giving full expression to the heart of the Spirit.

Elisha was clearly able to more readily discern the Voice of God as the minstrel played providing an atmosphere for the prophetic voice to flourish. I believe this will amplify in time with some services allowing the worshipers to continue as the anointed word flows through the prophetic leaders bringing the Word of the Lord in unison with the overflow of minstrel worship.

# INCREASE OF REVELATION AND RESTORATION: REVEAL, RECOVER & RESTORE

# Recover Everything

It is time God is going to recover everything lost. If you have gone through seasons of losing, get ready for breakthrough. In this Chapter we will examine the life of David and how he overcame tremendous adversity, you will discover how to be sustained as a bold overcomer! First I'll release vital revelation by speaking prophetically, and by those inspired words you will be strengthened to prevail victoriously against all odds. Also I will discuss worship, God's weapon of choice and how David's decision to worship and strengthen himself in his God caused him to triumph. Lastly we will continue studying the life of David and you will discover several crucial keys that will empower you to literally recover all that the enemy has stolen!

There's just so much that God is saying and yet He has given me a specific word, like a prophetic declaration, precisely for this hour! Not just a word from the Lord, but the word of the Lord. What I am about to share is something that God is saying to the church today, and believers will contend this year for its manifestation.

The word is actually Recover All! Words spoken to David before he became king during one of the most volatile periods of his life.

1 Samuel 30:8 And David enquired at the LORD, saying, Shall I pursue after this troop? shall I overtake them? And he

answered him, Pursue: for thou shalt surely overtake *them,* and without fail recover *all.*

When God spoke these weighty words to David he was in the middle of a grueling spiritual battle mixed with extremely nasty warfare in the natural. Because of where God wants to take us in terms of advancing the purposes of heaven on earth and the battle plan of the enemy to oppose this, we absolutely have to understand how to put all three commands into action and integrate them into our lives today. I believe that many of you are more than ready for this. After all, a good foundation has been laid on intimacy and the secret place (which we have discussed at length for some time now). This foundation is vital and it under girds several more prophetic revelations that I want to share with you today.

You know, as vital and hidden as intimacy and the secret place is there is something out there today that God wants to manifest among us. It's about worship! We are coming into a new season concerning powerful worship; a new season where the Lord is anointing the high praises and the victory in warfare that's released in the midst of worship. Worship is God's weapon of choice! And it doesn't end there! This is also a message of the call to war and what will we look like in this war? I believe that God is pouring out a fresh anointing and in this anointing God is releasing men and women with faces like lions! It's scriptural! That's what God is releasing! Men and women with faces like lions!

Now before I speak more about these prophetic revelations let's turn to God's Word. We're going to examine how these prophetic insights can be successfully applied in your life by studying the life of David and discovering how he prevailed against the enemy when his camp was raided by the Amalekites

1 Samuel 30:1, 2 And it came to pass, when David and his men were come to Ziklag on the third day, that the Amalekites had invaded the south, and Ziklag, and smitten Ziklag, and burned it with fire; And had taken the women captives, that *were* therein: they slew not any, either great or small, but carried *them* away, and went on their way.

David and his army were men of notoriety and so feared that when David was set to go to war against Saul with both the king of Gath whom he made an alliance with, and the Philistines, the Philistines would not allow him to take part in the coming battle.

1 Samuel 29:1-11 Now the Philistines gathered together all their armies to Aphek: and the Israelites pitched by a fountain which *is* in Jezreel. And the lords of the Philistines passed on by hundreds, and by thousands: but David and his men passed on in the rereward with Achish. Then said the princes of the Philistines, What *do* these Hebrews *here?* And Achish said unto the princes of the Philistines, *Is* not this David, the servant of Saul the king of Israel, which hath been with me these days, or these years, and I have found no fault in him since he fell *unto me* unto this day? And the princes of the Philistines were wroth with him; and the princes of the Philistines said unto him, Make this fellow return, that he may go again to his place which thou hast appointed him, and let him not go down with us to battle, lest in the battle he be an adversary to us: for wherewith should he reconcile himself unto his master? *should it* not *be* with the heads of these men? *Is* not this David, of whom they sang one to another in dances, saying, Saul slew his

thousands, and David his ten thousands? Then Achish called David, and said unto him, Surely, *as* the LORD liveth, thou hast been upright, and thy going out and thy coming in with me in the host *is* good in my sight: for I have not found evil in thee since the day of thy coming unto me unto this day: nevertheless the lords favour thee not. Wherefore now return, and go in peace, that thou displease not the lords of the Philistines. And David said unto Achish, But what have I done? and what hast thou found in thy servant so long as I have been with thee unto this day, that I may not go fight against the enemies of my lord the king? And Achish answered and said to David, I know that thou *art* good in my sight, as an angel of God: notwithstanding the princes of the Philistines have said, He shall not go up with us to the battle. Wherefore now rise up early in the morning with thy master's servants that are come with thee: and as soon as ye be up early in the morning, and have light, depart. So David and his men rose up early to depart in the morning, to return into the land of the Philistines. And the Philistines went up to Jezreel.

The Philistines did not know exactly where David's loyalty stood and they speculated that perhaps in the heat of battle he would turn on them to win back the favor of Saul. So David and his men were forced to pull out of the war and they returned to Ziklag, the place given (back) to them as a gift by the king of Gath.

1 Samuel 27:6 Then Achish gave him Ziklag that day: wherefore Ziklag pertaineth unto the kings of Judah unto this day.

Now Ziklag was a significant place or stronghold for David; and it also represents important prophetic symbolism

# INCREASE OF REVELATION AND RESTORATION:
## REVEAL, RECOVER & RESTORE

for us today. It was a place with an anointing and a call, located in the southern part of Judah. In fact, it was an inheritance of Judah.

Joshua 15:1 *This* then was the lot of the tribe of the children of Judah by their families; *even* to the border of Edom the wilderness of Zin southward *was* the uttermost part of the south coast.

Joshua 15:31 And Ziklag, and Madmannah, and Sansannah,

Therefore Ziklag actually belonged to the children of Judah, and this is very important because Judah means praise! So it was their city; an inheritance; where they lived and kept their possessions. But perhaps even more important than this, it was the place where the mighty men of valor came to David day by day to help him until there was a great army, like the army of God

1 Chronicles 12:20-22 As he went to Ziklag, there fell to him of Manasseh, Adnah, and Jozabad, and Jediael, and Michael, and Jozabad, and Elihu, and Zilthai, captains of the thousands that *were* of Manasseh. And they helped David against the band *of the rovers:* for they *were* all mighty men of valour, and were captains in the host. For at *that* time day by day there came to David to help him, until *it was* a great host, like the host of God.

Now you might be wondering what is the army of God? It's the army that's in heaven!

David wasn't king yet, but he was king in heart to these valiant men and he had a great army and it was like the army of God! We're talking mighty, mighty army here, and Ziklag was the great gathering place of the army that was like the army of God!

In modern-day terms, the prophetic significance for us (concerning Ziklag) is that it was apostolic, it was a training centre, it was a mission's base, and young men's hands were being trained for war there.

When David was forced to return from the war zone to his stronghold in Ziklag it was a bad, bad scene. The Amalekites had conducted a devastating raid while David and his mighty men were away. The enemy kidnapped all their loved ones and then burned their camp to the ground. The Bible says that when David and the mighty men saw the disaster, its full impact caused such tremendous grief that they were completely exhausted by it. Everyone's strength was gone as they deeply mourned for their loved ones, and David, once their hero, quickly lost his credibility because of that dire situation.

The people spoke of stoning him to death, and naturally David was greatly distressed. Here, these were the forerunners! The ones on the cutting edge of the day, and they had already been out in the battle and achieved many victories. These weren't just men, these were the mighty men. These were the leaders of the day. This was the next generation. This was the Joel's army! These mighty warriors all wanted to stone David!

What would you do in a great shaking like that? Here they were completely devastated, their stronghold was burned to the ground and their families were taken captive by the enemy. But let's make this even more personal. You come back and it's not just fire, it's not just a little battle, it's not just warfare, but it's everything that you are. When it's all gone, you have nothing left but ash. That happens in your life, in your family,

# INCREASE OF REVELATION AND RESTORATION:
## REVEAL, RECOVER & RESTORE

in your business, in your finances, your vision, the anointing on your life, God's call, your ministry, whatever it is.

David and his men experienced that Battle. Ziklag, an inheritance of Judah, a symbol of praise because Judah means praise, and out of praise comes triumph was burned to the ground with fire. Listen! The Lord told me: "Bill, this is what happens to the church that forgets the power that's in praise because it's out of praise that triumph comes. When there is no praise the city is burned with fire." The inheritance of Judah! Praise! That's what the devil is attacking in this hour our praise! But the good news is the Lord isn't going to let the enemy's plans triumph over us!

The Lord told me for those that would take up the weapon of praise this year, that they would be the ones that would have the greatest victory. Real praise this year will determine the victories that you have. I'm not just talking about a little worship and a little praise on Sunday or a little worship and praise in a conference or in your car. I'm talking about becoming a worship warrior!

There is a tremendous anointing and promise for those who take up the high weapon of praise this year.

Psalms 149:5, 6 Let the saints be joyful in glory: let them sing aloud upon their beds. *Let* the high *praises* of God *be* in their mouth, and a twoedged sword in their hand;

You see, this is the year of the sword, but there is something about the sword of the Lord in your hand and the high praises of God in your mouth. Why?

Psalms 149:7-9 To execute vengeance upon the heathen, *and* punishments upon the people; To bind their kings with chains, and their nobles with fetters of iron; To execute upon them the judgment written: this honour have all his saints. Praise ye the LORD.

God is going to breathe on that again. In the darkest hour that you face, the sword of the Lord in your hand will do its work by the high praises of God in your mouth.

Suddenly, great deliverances will come this year. It will be supernatural. With the "sound of an earthquake" instantly your loved ones will be free; the prison doors will open and all their bondage will come off just like those chains that fell to the ground around the apostle Paul and Silas when they released the high praises in jail.

Acts 16:25, 26 And at midnight Paul and Silas prayed, and sang praises unto God: and the prisoners heard them. And suddenly there was a great earthquake, so that the foundations of the prison were shaken: and immediately all the doors were opened, and every one's bands were loosed.

That's what we are going to see. The Lord is anointing the high praise and victorious warfare that's released in the midst of worship!

In David's great distress over the enemy's raid, coupled with the threats of death from his own men, the Bible says that "David strengthened himself in the Lord his God."

1 Samuel 30:6 And David was greatly distressed; for the people spake of stoning him, because the soul of all the people was grieved, every man for his sons and for his daughters: but David encouraged himself in the LORD his God.

David's inner determination to strengthen himself in his God, worked with God's determination to strengthen him in return! Something awesome was released to David when he worshipped God and purposed to press in to the Lord's heart in his time of tribulation. Because David's inner resolve lights the way for us today! It shines through like a powerful truth that we can grab a hold of! We need to make up our minds to press into God in the heat of the battle just like he did!

David's true grit also shines as a major key to becoming a worship warrior! And being a worship warrior is a crucial key to overcoming any weapon that has been formed against us! Selah!

I want to explain how David's determination to press in to God's heart in the heat of his intense spiritual battle caused him to make the right decisions; decisions that ultimately invited God's favor and counsel for war. I will outline several crucial keys that will help you discover why it is absolutely vital to strengthen yourself in God so that you will know what to do next when all hell breaks out against you.

It's war! This is an hour when we need to inquire of the Lord and stand in His counsel. Our stealth depends on this so that what hangs in the balance today comes through to complete breakthrough and victory. Have you noticed that the ordained destiny of God over many cities is in great jeopardy right now? In fact, God's destiny over your very life is probably in contention! We're in a battle!

Prophetically, in modern-day terms, Ziklag was an apostolic mission's base; day by day the-up-and-coming leaders came to the city. It was a training center; and young men's hands were being trained for war there. There was a school of supernatural ministry there.

They were mentoring interns and there was impartation. Men and women were being released from there all over the known world, equipped and anointed.

But in one day Ziklag's destiny hung in the balance. The city that symbolized praise was viciously leveled by Israel's enemies. And then, right after that raid, David faced one of the greatest spiritual battles of his entire life.

Many of you know how much I respect and identify with David. Talk about a hero of the faith! When he was about to be stoned by the men he loved, the mighty men of valor, he pulled aside to seek his God. The Amalekites had just ravaged and burned his camp to the ground Ziklag and kidnapped all the families staying there while David and his army were away. In their deep grief, the army turned on David. With the stench of acrid smoke still in their nostrils, they wanted to stone him. Both his credibility as their invincible leader, and his very life, were threatened.

The destiny of David's city, Ziklag, hung in the balance. And so did his personal destiny! There he stood at his ordained, divine, threshold. What was he going to do next? His choice would mark his future. He chose well! He set himself apart with his God in the secret place, and scripture says that "David strengthened himself in the Lord his God."

1 Samuel 30:6 And David was greatly distressed; for the people spake of stoning him, because the soul of all the people was grieved, every man for his sons and for his daughters: but David encouraged himself in the LORD his God.

Shut in with God, David's inner determination to strengthen himself in his God and to believe God's prophetic promises all worked together with God's determination to strengthen Him in return. David received all the true grit he needed to continue standing as Israel's great leader as well as receiving the spiritual sensitivity he needed to carry out a very important act.

What did he do? What was his action that carried the day? Scripture says that David spoke to Abiathar, the priest, "Please bring the ephod here to me."

1 Samuel 30:7 And David said to Abiathar the priest, Ahimelech's son, I pray thee, bring me hither the ephod. And Abiathar brought thither the ephod to David.

David identified with this holy, priestly garment because it symbolized the true intentions of his heart his deep love and respect for God. Also, he knew from past experience that the ephod represented counsel and advice.

1 Samuel 30:9-12 So David went, he and the six hundred men that *were* with him, and came to the brook Besor, where those that were left behind stayed. But David pursued, he and four hundred men: for two hundred abode behind, which were so faint that they could not go over the brook Besor. And they found an Egyptian in the field, and brought him to David, and gave him bread, and he did eat; and they made him drink water; And they gave him a piece of a cake of figs, and two clusters of raisins: and when he had eaten, his spirit came again to him: for he had eaten no bread, nor drunk *any* water, three days and three nights.

Wisely, he asked for the ephod. He took off his armor, and with great reverence, the man after God's own heart put on the priestly garment.

Desperate times called for desperate measures and he continued to strengthen himself in the Lord, pressing into God's heart. He had to know what to do next. He was warring in the spirit, in worship, as a true worship warrior. When he knew he caught God's eye and had His ear, David inquired of the Lord "Shall I pursue this troop? Shall I overtake them?" Immediately God answered, "Pursue, for you shall surely overtake them and without fail recover all."

1 Samuel 30:8 And David enquired at the LORD, saying, Shall I pursue after this troop? shall I overtake them? And he answered him, Pursue: for thou shalt surely overtake *them,* and without fail recover *all.*

You are standing at your own personal divine threshold. You may be contending for your family, the anointing, faith, vision, ministry, and your city, whatever it is. God is declaring to you today: "Pursue, overtake and without fail you are going to recover all from the devil." If, like David, you come into the secret place as a worship warrior, you will be strengthened; and when you inquire of the Lord, your God will release to you His heavenly counsel. In your dark night of the soul, God will show you what to do next just like He did for David. I know this to be true because the Lord has done this for me.

As many of you know for more than a year, recently, I was in the process of the "dealings of God." For a while it felt like all my passion for God, vision, ministry, everything that I loved, was gone.

One day I had all the passion and vision and then the next day I heard the Lord say, "dark night of the soul," and immediately everything I loved about serving the Lord was gone. I could do nothing about it, because it was God's will. When God puts you on the rock and starts crushing you, grinding you to powder, it doesn't feel good.

All we can do in that hour of the dark night is to determine within ourselves to strengthen and encourage ourselves in the

Lord. If we don't, discouragement will defeat us. We've got to remember what God promised us. Listen! If we're going to be ready for what I believe God is releasing today, we've got to strengthen ourselves. And to do that we need a little shot of joy and oil, and wine and glory! That shot comes by taking to heart main keys:

### *Desiring God Above Everything Else*

Like the psalmist, all our desire will be for God; our souls will pant and thirst for the living God.

Psalms 42:1 **To the chief Musician, Maschil, for the sons of Korah.** As the hart panteth after the water brooks, so panteth my soul after thee, O God.

Psalms 63:1-11 **A Psalm of David, when he was in the wilderness of Judah.** O God, thou *art* my God; early will I seek thee: my soul thirsteth for thee, my flesh longeth for thee in a dry and thirsty land, where no water is; To see thy power and thy glory, so *as* I have seen thee in the sanctuary. Because thy lovingkindness *is* better than life, my lips shall praise thee. Thus will I bless thee while I live: I will lift up my hands in thy name. My soul shall be satisfied as *with* marrow and fatness; and my mouth shall praise *thee* with joyful lips: When I remember thee upon my bed, *and* meditate on thee in the *night* watches. Because thou hast been my help, therefore in the shadow of thy wings will I rejoice. My soul followeth hard after thee: thy right hand upholdeth me. But those *that* seek my soul, to destroy *it,* shall go into the lower parts of the earth. They shall fall by the sword: they shall be a portion for foxes.

But the king shall rejoice in God; every one that sweareth by him shall glory: but the mouth of them that speak lies shall be stopped.

1 Timothy 1:18, 19 This charge I commit unto thee, son Timothy, according to the prophecies which went before on thee, that thou by them mightest war a good warfare; Holding faith, and a good conscience; which some having put away concerning faith have made shipwreck:

Building ourselves up in our most holy faith, praying in the Holy Spirit, not forgetting the hidden power of praying in tongues.

Jude 1:20 But ye, beloved, building up yourselves on your most holy faith, praying in the Holy Ghost,

Facing the giants that almost took us out in the past.

Judges 20:1-48 Then all the children of Israel went out, and the congregation was gathered together as one man, from Dan even to Beersheba, with the land of Gilead, unto the LORD in Mizpeh. And the chief of all the people, *even* of all the tribes of Israel, presented themselves in the assembly of the people of God, four hundred thousand footmen that drew sword. (Now the children of Benjamin heard that the children of Israel were gone up to Mizpeh.) Then said the children of Israel, Tell *us,* how was this wickedness? And the Levite, the husband of the woman that was slain, answered and said, I came into Gibeah that *belongeth* to Benjamin, I and my concubine, to lodge. And the men of Gibeah rose against me, and beset the house round about upon me by night, *and* thought to have slain me: and my concubine have they forced, that she is dead. And I took my concubine, and cut her in pieces, and sent her throughout all the country of the inheritance of Israel: for they have committed lewdness and folly in Israel. Behold, ye *are* all children of Israel; give here your advice and counsel. And all the people arose as one man, saying, We will not any *of us* go

# INCREASE OF REVELATION AND RESTORATION: REVEAL, RECOVER & RESTORE

to his tent, neither will we any *of us* turn into his house. But now this *shall be* the thing which we will do to Gibeah; *we will go up* by lot against it; And we will take ten men of an hundred throughout all the tribes of Israel, and an hundred of a thousand, and a thousand out of ten thousand, to fetch victual for the people, that they may do, when they come to Gibeah of Benjamin, according to all the folly that they have wrought in Israel. So all the men of Israel were gathered against the city, knit together as one man. And the tribes of Israel sent men through all the tribe of Benjamin, saying, What wickedness *is* this that is done among you? Now therefore deliver *us* the men, the children of Belial, which *are* in Gibeah, that we may put them to death, and put away evil from Israel. But the children of Benjamin would not hearken to the voice of their brethren the children of Israel: But the children of Benjamin gathered themselves together out of the cities unto Gibeah, to go out to battle against the children of Israel. And the children of Benjamin were numbered at that time out of the cities twenty and six thousand men that drew sword, beside the inhabitants of Gibeah, which were numbered seven hundred chosen men. Among all this people *there were* seven hundred chosen men lefthanded; every one could sling stones at an hair *breadth,* and not miss. And the men of Israel, beside Benjamin, were numbered four hundred thousand men that drew sword: all these *were* men of war. And the children of Israel arose, and went up to the house of God, and asked counsel of God, and said, Which of us shall go up first to the battle against the children of Benjamin? And the LORD said, Judah *shall go up* first. And the children of Israel rose up in the morning, and encamped against Gibeah. And the men of Israel went out to battle against Benjamin; and the men of Israel put themselves in array to fight against them at Gibeah. And the children of Benjamin came forth out of Gibeah, and destroyed down to the ground of the Israelites that day twenty and two thousand men. And the people the men of Israel encouraged themselves, and set their battle again in array in the place where they put themselves in array the first day. (And the children of Israel went up and wept before the LORD until even, and asked counsel of the LORD, saying, Shall I go up again to battle against the children of Benjamin my brother? And the LORD said, Go up against him.) And the children of Israel came near against the children of Benjamin the second day. And Benjamin went forth against them out of Gibeah the second day, and destroyed down to the ground of the children of Israel again eighteen thousand men; all these drew the sword. Then all the children of Israel, and all the people, went up, and came unto the house of God, and wept, and sat there before the LORD, and fasted that day until even, and offered burnt offerings and peace offerings before the LORD. And the children of Israel enquired of the LORD, (for the ark of the covenant of God *was* there in those days, And Phinehas, the son of Eleazar, the son of Aaron, stood before it in those days,) saying, Shall I yet again go out to battle against the children of Benjamin my brother, or shall I cease? And the LORD said, Go up; for to morrow I will deliver them into thine hand. And Israel set liers in wait round about Gibeah. And the children of Israel went up against the children of Benjamin on the third day, and put themselves in array against Gibeah, as at other times. And the children of Benjamin went out against the people, *and* were drawn away from the city; and they began to smite of the people, *and* kill, as at other times, in the highways, of which one goeth up to the house of God, and the other to Gibeah in the field, about thirty men of Israel. And the children of Benjamin said, They *are* smitten down before us, as at the first. But the children of Israel said, Let us flee, and draw them from the city unto the highways. And all the men of Israel rose up out of their place, and put themselves in array at Baaltamar: and the liers in wait of Israel came forth out of their places, *even* out of the meadows of Gibeah. And there came against Gibeah ten thousand chosen men out of all Israel, and the battle was sore: but they knew not that evil *was* near them. And the LORD smote Benjamin before Israel: and the children of Israel destroyed of the Benjamites that day twenty and five thousand and an hundred men: all these drew the sword. So the children of Benjamin saw that they were smitten: for the men of Israel gave place to the Benjamites, because they trusted unto the liers in wait which they had set beside Gibeah. And the liers in wait hasted, and rushed upon Gibeah; and the liers in wait drew *themselves* along, and smote all the city with the edge of the sword. Now there was an appointed sign between the men of Israel and the liers in wait, that they should make a great flame with smoke rise up out of the city. And when the men of Israel retired in the battle, Benjamin began to smite *and* kill of the men of Israel about thirty persons: for they said, Surely they are smitten down before us, as *in* the first battle. But when the flame began to arise up out of the city with a pillar of smoke, the Benjamites looked behind them, and, behold, the flame of the city ascended up to heaven. And when the men of Israel turned again, the men of Benjamin were amazed: for they saw that evil was come upon them. Therefore they turned *their backs* before the men of Israel unto the way of the wilderness; but the battle overtook them; and them which *came* out of the cities they destroyed in the midst of them. *Thus* they inclosed the Benjamites round about, *and* chased them, *and* trode them down with ease over against Gibeah toward the sunrising. And there fell of Benjamin eighteen thousand men; all these *were* men of valour. And they turned and fled toward the wilderness unto the rock of Rimmon: and they gleaned of them in the highways five thousand men; and pursued hard after them unto Gidom, and slew two thousand men of them. So that all which fell that day of Benjamin were twenty and five thousand men that drew the sword; all these *were* men of valour. But six hundred men turned and fled to the wilderness unto the rock Rimmon, and abode in the rock Rimmon four months. And the men of Israel turned again upon the children of Benjamin, and smote them with the edge of the sword, as well the men of *every* city, as the beast, and all that came to hand: also they set on fire all the cities that they came to.

By receiving and applying these keys in your life, you will be almost or nearly ready to go to war and plunder the enemy's camp! But before you go, God wants to complete your preparation by pouring out a new fresh anointing on you!

In this anointing the Lord wants to terrorize the enemy by giving you a face like a lion! Look at this! One division of David's army was from the tribe of Gad (Gadites). They were eleven "mighty men of valor, men trained for battle, who could handle shield and spear, whose faces were like the faces of lions, and were as swift as gazelles on the mountains."

1 Chronicles 12:8 And of the Gadites there separated themselves unto David into the hold to the wilderness men

of might, *and* men of war *fit* for the battle, that could handle shield and buckler, whose faces *were like* the faces of lions, and *were* as swift as the roes upon the mountains; They were the fiercest tribe in all of Israel. These men had faces like lions. Now, that's an anointing! Scripture goes on to name each of the eleven warriors (Two of the warriors have the same name, Jeremiah.)

Each warrior's name has a particular meaning with Strong's Number: Ezer/Ezar: treasure #687; Obadiah: servant #5662/#5647; Eliab: God (of his) Father #446; Mishmannah: fatness #4925; Jeremiah: appointed by God (Jer. 1:4); Attai: timely fit #6262/#6261; Eliel: strength, mighty #447/#410; Johanan: merciful #3110, #3076, #2603; Elzabad: God has bestowed #443; Machbannai (Machannite): native of the land #4344, #4343. Nine definitions are taken from Strong's Exhaustive Concordance of the Bible.

These were the most ferocious and yet they were men of mercy; they were servants. These were fearsome warriors and yet they were a help and a treasure. Though they were the wildest, they knew the Father's love and they knew God's appointed time. They were the most aggressive and yet they knew how to trust in the Lord and that God would provide for them. Men with faces like lions! Men that God called!

I believe that God wants to anoint us with faces like lions, with a fierce spirit within us like the men of the tribe of Gad. Begin to cry out to the Lord for this anointing!! It will empower you with a godly vengeance to pursue, overtake, and recover all that the enemy has robbed from you!

Pursue literally means to advance. It means to participate. Church, this is an hour to participate! Equally, it means to search for and pursue with hostile intent. Listen! This is the year to pursue your enemy with hostile intent. It means to catch or capture something with persistence.

God is saying the word for 2010-2015 this time is PURSUE! But the battle is not going to be easy. God wants to give you a holy persistence that will empower you to never give up!

Overtake means to achieve a level once obtained that you've lost, and not only catch up, but to pass it and take it by surprise. How about you? Do you have some regrets over some of the decisions you have made? You were set back. This is the year to catch up, to redeem the time, and to overtake.

Recover all means to regain, regain as in former condition, to cover anew, and to re-gather one's position.

Back to David! As soon as David received God's command to attack the Amalekites, he proceeded immediately to pursue and hunt down his enemies.

1 Samuel 30:8-16 And David enquired at the LORD, saying, Shall I pursue after this troop? shall I overtake them? And he answered him, Pursue: for thou shalt surely overtake *them*, and without fail recover *all*. So David went, he and the six hundred men that *were* with him, and came to the brook Besor, where those that were left behind stayed. But David pursued, he and four hundred men: for two hundred abode behind, which were so faint that they could not go over the brook Besor. And they found an Egyptian in the field, and brought him to David, and gave him bread, and he did eat; and they made him drink water; And they gave him a piece of a cake of figs, and two clusters of raisins: and when he had eaten, his spirit came again to him: for he had eaten no bread, nor

# INCREASE OF REVELATION AND RESTORATION:
## REVEAL, RECOVER & RESTORE

drunk *any* water, three days and three nights. And David said unto him, To whom *belongest* thou? and whence *art* thou? And he said, I *am* a young man of Egypt, servant to an Amalekite; and my master left me, because three days agone I fell sick. We made an invasion *upon* the south of the Cherethites, and upon *the coast* which *belongeth* to Judah, and upon the south of Caleb; and we burned Ziklag with fire. And David said to him, Canst thou bring me down to this company? And he said, Swear unto me by God, that thou wilt neither kill me, nor deliver me into the hands of my master, and I will bring thee down to this company. And when he had brought him down, behold, *they were* spread abroad upon all the earth, eating and drinking, and dancing, because of all the great spoil that they had taken out of the land of the Philistines, and out of the land of Judah.

Finding them spread all over the land celebrating because of the great spoil they had stolen, David and his mighty army swiftly attacked and overtook them. It was a long battle.

1 Samuel 30:17-20 And David smote them from the twilight even unto the evening of the next day: and there escaped not a man of them, save four hundred young men, which rode upon camels, and fled. And David recovered all that the Amalekites had carried away: and David rescued his two wives. And there was nothing lacking to them, neither small nor great, neither sons nor daughters, neither spoil, nor any *thing* that they had taken to them: David recovered all. And David took all the flocks and the herds, *which* they drave before those *other* cattle, and said, This *is* David's spoil.

How many of you want to recover everything that has been lost in the battle, lost to the devil. How many of you want that victory to be your promise for this year? I want you to receive this. Lift your hands up.

There's something about praise! There's something about the secret place and pressing in as a worship warrior! There's something about the ephod and inquiring of the Lord. There is something about strengthening and encouraging you in the Lord and saying, "I'm going to have the victory! I am not going to be discouraged and the only way I am going to remain strong is by taking up the ephod."

This is an hour in which God is releasing sweet companionship. He wants friendship and fellowship with you. It's also an hour in which He is releasing that fierce spirit upon men and women so that they will battle persistently, never giving up, shutting up, or letting up until they recover all! God wants you to fight for the destiny over your cities and over your lives! He wants to make your faces like lions!

It's time to pray and praise the Lord! Just lift up your voice wherever you are right now. (If you want breakthrough do it now) I feel a spontaneous release of the Spirit of God. God wants us to give praise to the Lion of the tribe of Judah, JESUS CHRIST, who is releasing an anointing of warfare in the high praises so that we would be like the mighty men, like the army of God, fully equipped to pursue the enemy, overtake, and recover all! This is God's will for you TAKE IT IN JESUS' NAME!!!

# INCREASE OF REVELATION AND RESTORATION: REVEAL, RECOVER & RESTORE

# Restoration

This is the time God is speaking RESTORE RESTORE RESTORE! In this Chapter I want to set the bar a few notches higher by sharing about the ultimate restoration. Then you'll learn about God's intention to release a new anointing for great deliverance from destruction and long standing bondage through the authority and power inherent in His word. You'll also discover how high praise and deliverance go hand in hand and how your identity in Christ influences your level of godly authority. In the last part of this chapter, I will impart more truth about restoration, you'll not only see restoration happening in your own life, and you'll also be prepared to facilitate it in the lives of those around you.

Luke 18:17 Verily I say unto you, Whosoever shall not receive the kingdom of God as a little child shall in no wise enter therein.

### *Unbelief has to go!*

BY INCREASING THE AUTHORITY of the spoken word, the power and preaching of the word, and it's not only going to bring deliverance from demonic bondage, it's going to bring restoration. In America, we see less of a manifestation because the demons tend to hide in the spirit of **religion**! Now don't miss this. The Lord told me that the spirit of religion is the greatest devil that's the spirit Jesus dealt with in Israel. It always has a form of godliness that denies the power of God. It always hides under the disguise of religion.

Despite that, no matter where the demons try to hide, God spoke to me about the anointing that's going to set the captives free the anointing that both removes the yoke and the burden by the work of the Spirit and the work of the anointing. There's going to be an anointing of great deliverance not just "deliverance," great deliverance as God sends forth His word; and the very authority and power of the spoken word will deliver people from destruction. Remember, Jesus spoke the word and cast out spirits with the word; in the instant that someone would hear the word of God, the anointing on the word would set that person free from perhaps years of bondage.

Having said that, I realize that there are some good models and some good courses that teach and train on deliverance and healing. We thank God for it all. But we're going to see God's power come swiftly and there will be instantaneous deliverances.

1 John 3:8 He that committeth sin is of the devil; for the devil sinneth from the beginning. For this purpose the Son of God was manifested, that he might destroy the works of the devil.

A meaning of the word destroy is to loose and undo. Yes, Jesus wants to loose and undo us from the works of the devil!

So, the fear, the rejection, the eating disorder, whatever is in your mindset that's plagued you or your family, generational curses, addictions whatever that one thing is that you've struggled with over the years the Lord told me there's going to be a release of the anointing that's going to bring deliverance. Not just from demonic bondage. I'm talking about the strongholds, mindsets, belief systems, insecurities, and fear . . . those people in your family sons, daughters, and drug addict's situations you've been praying about, things that have burdened you. Your cry is being heard by the Lord who delivers! God is breathing on Psalm 40.

Psalms 40:1-3 **To the chief Musician, A Psalm of David.** I waited patiently for the LORD; and he inclined unto me, and heard my cry. He brought me up also out of an horrible pit, out of the miry clay, and set my feet upon a rock, *and* established my goings. And he hath put a new song in my mouth, *even* praise unto our God: many shall see *it,* and fear, and shall trust in the LORD.

Verse 3 speaks of a new song, praise to our God many will see it and fear.

Many will see what? The praise! The new song! They're going to see it and fear; they're going to hear it. The deliverance is connected to the anointing that's on the praise, the high praise, and when we reach those realms of high praise, there's going to be deliverance. God said, "This year I'm taking people, not just out of the pit, I'm taking them out of the horrible pit, years of trauma, years of abuse. Whatever it is, He's going to begin to hear your cry for deliverance and bring spontaneous supernatural intervention.

I don't know why, but whatever the reason, prophetically, God has an appointed time. We sometimes hear incredible testimonies of people who just seem to go from outer darkness and then they get set free. Then, for others, it seems like it takes 25 years to unwrap the grave clothes, and they're still working it out. In fact, some believers are always in a season of inner healing. I mean, they're always wounded and offended and need an inner healing. Where is the victorious triumphant church! So I tell them to get that victim thing off their head and win some souls, get back to that, and preach the gospel!

God told me that conquering is a mindset.

1 Corinthians 15:57 But thanks *be* to God, which giveth us the victory through our Lord Jesus Christ.

In fact, victory is a key word for this year. However, our circumstances often don't reflect that, and there are times when we shrink back. In the day of battle, we sometimes turn back because the last time we went for it things got too hot, and now we're not so eager to run out there again. One way or the other, we walk with a mindset! What's yours? People are still in the mode like; I'm not ready for the battle." But there's something in me that goes, "Yeah! Bring it on!"

You know what? We've got to think victoriously "we are more than conquerors"

Romans 8:37 Nay, in all these things we are more than conquerors through him that loved us.

1 John 4:4 Ye are of God, little children, and have overcome them: because greater is he that is in you, than he that is in the world.

We have been given power and authority to trample on serpents and scorpions, and over all the power of the enemy, and nothing shall by any means hurt us.

Luke 10:19 Behold, I give unto you power to tread on serpents and scorpions, and over all the power of the enemy: and nothing shall by any means hurt you.

With a mandate like that, do you really know who you are? Better yet, do you really know who Christ is in you? What kind of Jesus is living on the inside of you? I say that because there comes the day when we just have to get our soul in check. "I'm going to hope in God. Get it together, soul. No more wallowing!" Hey! Just kick your soul's butt! (Yes I said it and it is time ministers speak up) "What do you think you're doing, soul? Do you know who you are?

Did you read your Bible lately? What do you think you're doing, mountain? Do you know who you are, mountain? You shall become a plain!" Talking to your soul like that brings it in line with your destiny!

Taking my life as an example, as God began to shed light on my destiny.

Luke 1:76-79 And thou, child, shalt be called the prophet of the Highest: for thou shalt go before the face of the Lord to prepare his ways; To give knowledge of salvation unto his people by the remission of their sins, Through the tender mercy of our God; whereby the dayspring from on high hath visited us, To give light to them that sit in darkness and *in* the shadow of death, to guide our feet into the way of peace.

John 20:21 Then said Jesus to them again, Peace *be* unto you: as *my* Father hath sent me, even so send I you.

It's time to get back to the simplicity of the gospel and our call.

Within this fresh anointing He is inviting us to partner with Him in the authority and power inherent in His word not only for personal deliverance, but also for setting the captives free. Wow! That's good news!

Isaiah 61:1, 2 The Spirit of the Lord GOD *is* upon me; because the LORD hath anointed me to preach good tidings unto the meek; he hath sent me to bind up the brokenhearted, to proclaim liberty to the captives, and the opening of the prison to *them that are* bound; To proclaim the acceptable year of the LORD, and the day of vengeance of our God; to comfort all that mourn;

The Spirit of the Lord God is upon Me "to proclaim liberty to the captives" and "to proclaim the acceptable year of the Lord." In a different Bible translation "the acceptable year of the Lord" is rendered: "to proclaim the year of the Lord's favor."

There is an anointing available to you and me to proclaim, prophesy, decree, and declare a season of favor! The impact of this anointing really comes into position once we come to understand what it means to be a servant of the Lord.

Being God's servant means there is an authority available to us under or in the anointing, that in the moment we decree "favor" or just say the word "favor" over someone's life (in the anointing), they have to come into favor! I want to emphasize "under or in the anointing" because it's in moments of an open heaven, when there's a realm of the spirit, that we can make decrees that change destinies through the spoken word. Favor goes hand in hand with deliverance and restoration—which describe what "Jubilee" is. Biblically, in Leviticus Chapter 25, Jubilee means the cancellation of all debt, the release of property, the release of slaves, and more. For us today, it means the return of our sons and daughters, the release of our investments, cancellation of debts for us and our family, and liberation from bondage and oppression.

With that in mind, part of my ministry responsibility today as a preacher is to proclaim Jubilee a prophetic proclamation of liberty and freedom that will shift believers into a realm of the power of God's Spirit that makes everything that's out of order, come into order and freedom.

Moving along in verse 2 of Isaiah 61, "To proclaim the acceptable year of the LORD, and the day of vengeance of our God" Vengeance is a "settling of scores" and it's directly connected to vindication and justice! As servants of the Lord, the Spirit of the Lord is upon us to proclaim the day of vengeance of our God; and when we do, we can literally say "justice," "vindication," "the vengeance of God" and the moment we make that decree under the anointing, everything that is deemed by the courts of heaven as unjust, gets overturned.

Next, I want to outline some different aspects involved in restoration and then, with that foundation laid, we'll go back to prophetic declarations, focusing on authoritative command in spiritual warfare.

So let's take a look at the rest of verse 2: "To comfort all who mourn" and then examine verse 3: "To console those who mourn in Zion, to give them beauty for ashes." I love those verses the anointing to make something beautiful out of what's just ash to give beauty for ashes. It's called the holy exchange.

Your business, your marriage, finances, your self worth; whatever it is in your life that's nothing but ash, there is an anointing to replace it with beauty. God always takes the ashes and makes something beautiful! Isn't that a great anointing? There are people anointed to bring an exchange your ashes for His beauty. Talk about a makeover!

It goes on in verse 3: "The oil of joy for mourning, the garment of praise for the spirit of heaviness..." Verse 4: "They will rebuild the ancient ruins and restore the places long devastated; they will renew the ruined cities that have been devastated for generations" (NIV). It's the anointing to restore everything that's been lost in a previous generation all the old mantles, all the old anointing there's literally an anointing, to raise up, repair, and restore.

Actually, did you know that it's one thing to loose and undo the work of the devil it's one thing to be set free but it's another thing to have God restore back in your life all the damage that was done because of the oppression of the enemy?

In other words, just think for a moment about the alcoholic that gets set free, and we thank God for that. But what about all the aftermath the damage that the alcoholism did to the children and others or the drug addict that's now free, but the family is still broke?

The fact is, there are testimonies of people that have come into notable freedom, yet there still remain lingering negative consequences. But biblical restoration cuts off those negative consequences! That's because, when God restores, one: He brings an increase; two: He multiplies beyond where you were; and three: He adds the extra, making it better than it was before. Look at Job. When God restored Job, He gave him double. In fact, you cannot be touched by the anointing of restoration and, for example, just get your money back at the same measure. It's not just recovery of a former condition. No! You're not going back to a former state. You're going back to better! I mean, when God restores, say double, it's everything double life, joy, and revelation, and much more! For instance,

# INCREASE OF REVELATION AND RESTORATION:
## REVEAL, RECOVER & RESTORE

in the Bible we see that if harm came to someone or something was stolen, God commanded that the return be greater than what was plundered or robbed. Occasionally the return would "one for one," but almost every single time the return was more than that a double blessing, or four or five times greater.

Exodus 22:1 If a man shall steal an ox, or a sheep, and kill it, or sell it; he shall restore five oxen for an ox, and four sheep for a sheep.

Exodus 22:4 If the theft be certainly found in his hand alive, whether it be ox, or ass, or sheep; he shall restore double.

Leviticus 6:5 Or all that about which he hath sworn falsely; he shall even restore it in the principal, and shall add the fifth part more thereto, *and* give it unto him to whom it appertaineth, in the day of his trespass offering.

Leviticus 22:14 And if a man eat *of* the holy thing unwittingly, then he shall put the fifth *part* thereof unto it, and shall give *it* unto the priest with the holy thing.

Proverbs 6:31 But *if* he be found, he shall restore sevenfold; he shall give all the substance of his house.

There is a "sevenfold" principle involved in restoration. God wants to bless you with an increase and to command the thief to give back sevenfold!

Thus says the LORD: In an acceptable time I have heard You, and in the day of salvation I have helped You; I will preserve You and give You as a covenant to the people, to restore the earth, to cause them to inherit the desolate heritages; That You may say to the prisoners, Go forth, to those who are in darkness, show yourselves. They shall feed along the roads, and their pastures shall be on all desolate heights"

We're talking about Jesus. And we're talking about you and me and the anointing of restoration to restore the earth, and to cause people to inherit the desolate heritages, or the inheritances that they've lost.

Then it goes on, "That You may say to the prisoners, Go forth, to those who are in darkness, show yourselves.'" Wow! Exodus 14:16 But lift thou up thy rod, and stretch out thine hand over the sea, and divide it: and the children of Israel shall go on dry *ground* through the midst of the sea.

"Actually just before God told Moses to stretch forth his rod, he said, "Why do you cry to Me Tell the children of Israel to go forward" (v.15)." Can you imagine if you were praying about healing and God said to you, "What are you doing crying to me?" I mean we'd be devastated, wouldn't we?

The Apostle Peter got out there and did something!

Acts 3:6 Then Peter said, Silver and gold have I none; but such as I have give I thee: In the name of Jesus Christ of Nazareth rise up and walk.

That crippled man walked; because of the power of God, yes, and it flowed through Peter because he knew his authority in God's kingdom.

Likewise, you'll know your authority the day that you accept who you are in Christ, what God called you to, and who Christ is in you. Then, you'll live accordingly, because there is a place at times, in the kingdom, where we need to begin to move with authority, make a command, make a decree, be aggressive and say to the one who sits in darkness, "Show yourself." Say to the one who is confined, "Come out of the prison; come out prisoner!"

## INCREASE OF REVELATION AND RESTORATION: REVEAL, RECOVER & RESTORE

Isaiah 42:22 But this *is* a people robbed and spoiled; *they are* all of them snared in holes, and they are hid in prison houses: they are for a prey, and none delivereth; for a spoil, and none saith, Restore.

Church! Be the one that says, "Restore!" Believe that He wants to give you the anointing for the ministry of restoration, to repair people's lives and rebuild what was ruined. Truly, today, God is making a way for those held in bondage to be set free great deliverance—great restoration!

For the hour is upon us to co-labor with Him for complete restoration, not only in our own lives but also in the lives of those around us. Remember,

Ecclesiastes 3:1 To every *thing there is* a season, and a time to every purpose under the heaven:

Let's seize the hour! Come on, now! Come on church!

# Travail of the Soul

The Holy Spirit wants us to be stirred to deep prayer and intercession known as travail. In this Chapter, we will discuss what it takes to co-labor with the Holy Spirit to bring in the harvest and how to be engaged in deep intercession to release souls into the kingdom of God. We're going to look at the serious subject of hell, as well as how to pray and release souls and households from the grip of the enemy so people can be saved.

Choices! The Holy Spirit never goes against our will. God has given every Christian and every human being the freedom to choose. And when God wants to accomplish something, He makes His will known to us, the body of Christ, so that we have an opportunity to co-labor with Him. However, we have to decide whether or not we're going to obey each call or assignment that the Lord wants to give us.

At this very moment as these words are being heard, the Lord is looking at mankind, His eyes blazing with love, His heart filled with a passionate longing for souls to be saved. Today, He is getting the ground ready so that many souls will be birthed into His kingdom. And He wants to properly prepare the "soil" of people's hearts so that they will respond to His message of love and salvation. The right kind of preparation is crucial in the battle to win souls. Therefore, God is asking us today if we are willing to co-labor with Him in preparing the way so that people will be saved. He's asking us if we will get "pregnant" with His burden and "pregnant" with His passion that souls would be saved. If we're willing, God wants to come and bring us into a deep level of intercession a deep level of prayer that will affect the spiritual atmosphere so that souls are eventually birthed into His kingdom. We call this intense level of intercession, "soul travail."

### *What is Soul Travail?*

I want to define what soul travail is.

First, (in the context of mankind's eternal soul), the word soul means: the spiritual nature of humans, regarded as immortal, separable from the body at death, and susceptible to happiness or misery in a future state—

The American Heritage® Dictionary.

Secondly, the word travail means: tribulation or agony; anguish and the labor of childbirth—

The American Heritage® Dictionary.

Soul travail happens after born-again believers conceive (by way of the Holy Spirit) God's burning desire that the lost would be saved. I'm talking about being pregnant in your spirit with the heart of God for the lost, pregnant with the heart of Jesus to win souls, pregnant with the burden of the Lord within your spirit to see souls set free, and pregnant with the vision of God for the harvest.

Soul travail isn't like a little prayer of blessing or like praying:

"God, save Allen." "God, save Randy." or "God, save my household." Rather, it's when we're so impregnated with the vision and the heart of God for people to receive Jesus Christ as

# INCREASE OF REVELATION AND RESTORATION:
## REVEAL, RECOVER & RESTORE

their Lord and Savior that we become broken under the burden of the Lord and His burden becomes our burden.

When this happens we literally fall on our face before God and begin to weep and travail in deep intercession for souls to be saved. (At the close of this Chapter I want to touch on the importance of releasing the burden back to God.)

One of the best illustrations of soul travail is found in the church in China. Let's think about the revival in China right now. It's been reported from one pastor in China that over 25,000 Chinese people a day are making decisions for Jesus Christ. How could such a huge number of people decide to follow the Lord Jesus? I believe the answer is directly connected to soul travail!

I watched a video of the church in China a while back and I saw the believers meeting together in underground churches in the morning. They were in heavy intercession for their friends and families to be saved. And some of the sights that I saw on the video were absolutely incredible. The Christians were so saturated with the vision and the heart of God that they went into intense labor and travail. The process of birthing those souls was an all consuming passion. They moved into that process because they were pregnant in the spirit with a great burden for the lost. They were literally shaking, with tears running down their face. It looked like agony, birthing, laboring and weeping for souls to be saved. It's plain to see that the believers in China have a burning vision ignited in their hearts that drives them to travail for souls. That's why there are 25,000 people a day being saved! What you see is what you get! The song, "Open the eyes of my heart, Lord..." is actually a reality for the believers in the underground church in China.

They see the harvest with the eyes of their heart and now they are getting a revival.

Are you provoked to jealousy?

I am!

I believe that just like China is birthing a great harvest, so can we, here in North America, if we are willing to pay the price to see it happen. Do you perceive and do you see the potential harvest not only on our continent, but also world-wide? Is what you see going to be what you get?

I want to try and help you begin today to lay hold of some keys and weapons that you can use in the heavenly places that will help you see your households released for salvation as well as multitudes birthed into the kingdom of God. I am a firm believer that if people are willing to spend time in fervent prayer, laboring and travailing in the secret place, then God's hand is going to move. The harvest will be reaped! So many times we think about some of the former mighty crusades that have taken place in certain places that brought revival.

Consider the Billy Graham crusades, for instance.

Thousands and thousands of people over the years have made decisions for Jesus Christ at Billy Graham crusades (and other evangelistic crusades). But what many believers don't realize is that much of the time before most crusades are launched in a City; there are one or two intercessors that are sent ahead into that particular city where the crusade will be held. They lock themselves up night and day in deep intercession, soul travail and they begin to birth the harvest by loosing souls in the spiritual realm.

In other words, they win the battle over souls in the spiritual realm first in secret. Then later at the crusade, victory

# INCREASE OF REVELATION AND RESTORATION:
## REVEAL, RECOVER & RESTORE

happens in the physical, natural realm because people are set free to make a decision for Jesus Christ! Their prayers help to bring the fuel for the fire that burns in those revival meetings.

You can be a powerful force in the hand of God to win those souls. This is for you, too! After you spend time in the secret place seeking the Lord, you will be able to see (perceive) with the eyes of your heart the vast number of souls that God wants to save.

What you see has great potential to be what you get! Your prayers, your soul travail, will help to make breakthroughs in the spiritual realm for your friends, family and city (to name just a few) so that the harvest completely ripens to the point that it can be reaped! Did you know that when you travail for the lost in prayer, you're going even further than fighting for them? You're actually birthing them into the kingdom of God because you're contending for their salvation in the spiritual realm (the heavens) and winning the battle there first.

I believe that God's favor is upon those who sacrifice themselves to travail in prayer for the salvation of souls. Although most of you, who take prayer for the lost seriously, aren't looking for recognition or rewards, I still want to say that the Lord has eternal rewards reserved for you in heaven.

Matthew 6:6 But thou, when thou prayest, enter into thy closet, and when thou hast shut thy door, pray to thy Father which is in secret; and thy Father which seeth in secret shall reward thee openly.

God cherishes every tear that drops when you pray.

Psalms 56:8 Thou tellest my wanderings: put thou my tears into thy bottle: *are they* not in thy book?

After all, it was Jesus who personally offered up both prayers and supplications with loud crying and tears to the Father.

Hebrews 5:7 Who in the days of his flesh, when he had offered up prayers and supplications with strong crying and tears unto him that was able to save him from death, and was heard in that he feared;

When He was seeking His Father's face in the garden of Gethsemane before His crucifixion, scripture tells us that Jesus' prayers were so passionate that His sweat became like drops of blood falling upon the ground.

Luke 22:44 And being in an agony he prayed more earnestly: and his sweat was as it were great drops of blood falling down to the ground.

I believe that if we are really moved from within with a holy desire to see people snatched out of the fire, if we cannot shed one tear, then I question whether or not we're actually pregnant with the heart of God.

Jude 1:23 And others save with fear, pulling *them* out of the fire; hating even the garment spotted by the flesh.

I've had times when the burden of the Lord has come on me and I've wept, groaned and moaned on the floor, broken, as God laid His burden on me for my city and for the multitudes of people in the world who do not know Him. It wasn't a fun time when this happened to me!

You know, we need to be ready to suffer through this stage of "pregnancy" when the travail and labor becomes so intense that we literally have to bear down with the birth pangs, groaning and weeping. We must not give up and leave our position in prayer at this critical point, because it's in this stage

# INCREASE OF REVELATION AND RESTORATION:
## REVEAL, RECOVER & RESTORE

of travail whereby we'll birth souls into the kingdom of God. And it's in this place that we need the Holy Spirit to help us so that we're moved by love to pray with compassion for the lost to be saved. Love avails much.

1 Corinthians 13:1-13 Though I speak with the tongues of men and of angels, and have not charity, I am become *as* sounding brass, or a tinkling cymbal. And though I have *the gift of* prophecy, and understand all mysteries, and all knowledge; and though I have all faith, so that I could remove mountains, and have not charity, I am nothing. And though I bestow all my goods to feed *the poor,* and though I give my body to be burned, and have not charity, it profiteth me nothing. Charity suffereth long, *and* is kind; charity envieth not; charity vaunteth not itself, is not puffed up, Doth not behave itself unseemly, seeketh not her own, is not easily provoked, thinketh no evil; Rejoiceth not in iniquity, but rejoiceth in the truth; Beareth all things, believeth all things, hopeth all things, endureth all things. Charity never faileth: but whether *there be* prophecies, they shall fail; whether *there be* tongues, they shall cease; whether *there be* knowledge, it shall vanish away. For we know in part, and we prophesy in part. But when that which is perfect is come, then that which is in part shall be done away. When I was a child, I spake as a child, I understood as a child, I thought as a child: but when I became a man, I put away childish things. For now we see through a glass, darkly; but then face to face: now I know in part; but then shall I know even as also I am known. And now abideth faith, hope, charity, these three; but the greatest of these *is* charity.

One of the main keys in birthing souls and seeing people saved is that we have to be touched by God's love and we have to be broken. And we need to love our neighbor as our self.

Matthew 19:19 Honour thy father and *thy* mother: and, Thou shalt love thy neighbour as thyself.

But what's first? The answer is to love God first.

Mark 12:30 And thou shalt love the Lord thy God with all thy heart, and with all thy soul, and with all thy mind, and with all thy strength: this *is* the first commandment.

That's our greatest call is to know Jesus Christ and out of relationship with Him we'll have a heart of love that moves us with compassion to see the lost saved. Then we won't be operating from a sense of duty and obligation. Jesus never ministered to people because it was something he had to do or because it was His "job." Rather He reached the lost because of His great love for them. I believe that Jesus' heart of love compelled Him to pray a great deal for mankind, and that He often did this in secret.

The Bible says that at various times he would spend time up on the mountain or he went into the wilderness and prayed.

Mark 1:35 And in the morning, rising up a great while before day, he went out, and departed into a solitary place, and there prayed.

Mark 6:46 And when he had sent them away, he departed into a mountain to pray.

Luke 5:16 And he withdrew himself into the wilderness, and prayed.

Luke 6:12 And it came to pass in those days, that he went out into a mountain to pray, and continued all night in prayer to God.

## INCREASE OF REVELATION AND RESTORATION:
## REVEAL, RECOVER & RESTORE

The love that Jesus has for mankind is illustrated so well in three passages of scripture one in the book of Matthew and the other two in the book of Luke and John.

Matthew 9:12, 13 But when Jesus heard *that,* he said unto them, They that be whole need not a physician, but they that are sick. But go ye and learn what *that* meaneth, I will have mercy, and not sacrifice: for I am not come to call the righteous, but sinners to repentance.

This statement is a direct reply that Jesus made to the religious clerics (the Pharisees), who accused Him of hanging out with the tax-gatherers and sinners. And He was! But His love for these tax gathers and sinners compelled Him to spend time with them and love-on them. Jesus knew how to fellowship with His new friends he reclined and ate with them. He wasn't sitting among them with a judgmental attitude. (Did you know that in Bible times, people actually reclined when they ate a meal?) And as Jesus hung out with them, scripture says that he was pulled away because a synagogue official's daughter had just died and he needed Jesus to raise her from the dead.

Matthew 9:18 While he spake these things unto them, behold, there came a certain ruler, and worshipped him, saying, My daughter is even now dead: but come and lay thy hand upon her, and she shall live.

So Jesus left the dinner party to help the official's family. However, on His way there a woman who had been ill for over a decade reached out to touch the fringe of His garment and she was instantly healed! It's like His healing virtue was never hindered from flowing to the sick because it poured freely from His heart of love. Nothing was stopping the flow not unforgiveness, not bitterness and not carnal judgmental attitudes.

Luke 19:10 For the Son of man is come to seek and to save that which was lost.

Luke 15:4-7 What man of you, having an hundred sheep, if he lose one of them, doth not leave the ninety and nine in the wilderness, and go after that which is lost, until he find it? And when he hath found *it,* he layeth *it* on his shoulders, rejoicing. And when he cometh home, he calleth together *his* friends and neighbours, saying unto them, Rejoice with me; for I have found my sheep which was lost. I say unto you, that likewise joy shall be in heaven over one sinner that repenteth, more than over ninety and nine just persons, which need no repentance.

John 4:6 Now Jacob's well was there. Jesus therefore, being wearied with *his* journey, sat thus on the well: *and* it was about the sixth hour.

John 4:10-24 Jesus answered and said unto her, If thou knewest the gift of God, and who it is that saith to thee, Give me to drink; thou wouldest have asked of him, and he would have given thee living water. The woman saith unto him, Sir, thou hast nothing to draw with, and the well is deep: from whence then hast thou that living water? Art thou greater than our father Jacob, which gave us the well, and drank thereof himself, and his children, and his cattle? Jesus answered and said unto her, Whosoever drinketh of this water shall thirst again: But whosoever drinketh of the water that I shall give him shall never thirst; but the water that I shall give him shall be in him a well of water springing up into everlasting life. The woman saith unto him, Sir, give me this water, that I thirst

# INCREASE OF REVELATION AND RESTORATION:
## REVEAL, RECOVER & RESTORE

not, neither come hither to draw. Jesus saith unto her, Go, call thy husband, and come hither. The woman answered and said, I have no husband. Jesus said unto her, Thou hast well said, I have no husband: For thou hast had five husbands; and he whom thou now hast is not thy husband: in that saidst thou truly. The woman saith unto him, Sir, I perceive that thou art a prophet. Our fathers worshipped in this mountain; and ye say, that in Jerusalem is the place where men ought to worship. Jesus saith unto her, Woman, believe me, the hour cometh, when ye shall neither in this mountain, nor yet at Jerusalem, worship the Father. Ye worship ye know not what: we know what we worship: for salvation is of the Jews. But the hour cometh, and now is, when the true worshippers shall worship the Father in spirit and in truth: for the Father seeketh such to worship him. God *is* a Spirit: and they that worship him must worship *him* in spirit and in truth.

But he was moved by love to speak with her and she was saved.

John 4:25-29 The woman saith unto him, I know that Messias cometh, which is called Christ: when he is come, he will tell us all things. Jesus saith unto her, I that speak unto thee am *he*. And upon this came his disciples, and marvelled that he talked with the woman: yet no man said, What seekest thou? or, Why talkest thou with her? The woman then left her waterpot, and went her way into the city, and saith to the men, Come, see a man, which told me all things that ever I did: is not this the Christ?

In the end Jesus stayed and hung out with the Samaritans for two more days and many of the Samaritans believed in Him.

John 4:39-42 And many of the Samaritans of that city believed on him for the saying of the woman, which testified, He told me all that ever I did. So when the Samaritans were come unto him, they besought him that he would tarry with them: and he abode there two days. And many more believed because of his own word; And said unto the woman, Now we believe, not because of thy saying: for we have heard *him* ourselves, and know that this is indeed the Christ, the Saviour of the world.

But it all began because God was so moved with compassion and love that He went out of his way. I believe that there is a fire; there is an anointing that can fall on us so that we are literally possessed with the heart of God. There is grace available from the Lord to bow before Him on our face, weeping and there is grace for us to be touched by the Holy Spirit to labor and travail for souls. (And God can take us out of our comfort zone and compel us by His Spirit to go into the streets to share the gospel with the lost. We'll be moved into evangelism.)

We can't have believers being stirred up to win souls out of duty and out of obligation because it's the Christian thing to do. But we can cry out and say, "Holy Spirit come and make us pregnant! Holy Spirit come and put inside of us the heart of God! Holy Spirit come and break us like You are broken for souls to be saved. Help us to travail for souls." Will we go out of our way to travail for lost souls to be saved? Sometimes going out of our way will mean that we'll experience some suffering. Are we prepared to pay that price too?

There is another cost concerning soul travail that we need to discuss. Let's begin by examining the ministry of intercession that Jesus had. You know that Jesus, in order for Him to be the greatest intercessor, to be the greatest High Priest, to have the ministry forever of intercession.

Hebrews 4:14 Seeing then that we have a great high priest, that is passed into the heavens, Jesus the Son of God, let us hold fast *our* profession.

Hebrews 5:1-10 For every high priest taken from among men is ordained for men in things *pertaining* to God, that he may offer both gifts and sacrifices for sins: Who can have compassion on the ignorant, and on them that are out of the way; for that he himself also is compassed with infirmity. And by reason hereof he ought, as for the people, so also for himself, to offer for sins. And no man taketh this honour unto himself, but he that is called of God, as *was* Aaron. So also Christ glorified not himself to be made an high priest; but he that said unto him, Thou art my Son, to day have I begotten thee. As he saith also in another *place,* Thou *art* a priest for ever after the order of Melchisedec. Who in the days of his flesh, when he had offered up prayers and supplications with strong crying and tears unto him that was able to save him from death, and was heard in that he feared; Though he were a Son, yet learned he obedience by the things which he suffered; And being made perfect, he became the author of eternal salvation unto all them that obey him; Called of God an high priest after the order of Melchisedec.

He had to identify with us. Therefore, He gave up His glory in heaven and became God in the flesh and took on a human body. What a drastic change! He gave up the glory and power in the heavenly realm and came down to earth as the Son of God, with no reputation. When He took on human flesh just like ours, He was tempted as we are tempted, yet without sin. He knew then, and He knows now, what we're going through. He identified with our human condition and He saw first-hand how needy and lost we are. In fact, because of His personal identification , He could become our High Priest and Intercessor.

You know, we need to be able to identify with the lost, too. Perhaps we need to remember what our lives were like before when we were blind and walking in darkness. Because afterwards we'll have more passion and feel the urgency to see that lost souls find Jesus Christ. God wants us to be moved with a burning heart for the lost to be saved! When we allow the Holy Spirit to take us into a place of identification, we will actually identify with the plight of the lost to the point that our heart and emotions become involved.

At this point we need to persevere and allow ourselves to move into prayer in a deeper and deeper way, travailing for the salvation of souls. However, it is also important when we're engaged in soul travail to remember to completely release the burden back to the Lord after prayer. We're not meant to be engaged in soul travail all the time! Yes, we co-labor with the Holy Spirit in travailing for souls to be saved, but we need to release the burden back to God.

Soul travail is an impassioned deep level of intercession (prayer) that affects the spiritual atmosphere so that the lost can hear the gospel and make a decision to receive Jesus Christ as their Lord and Savior.

Now we will begin discussing an extremely serious subject hell.

# INCREASE OF REVELATION AND RESTORATION:
## REVEAL, RECOVER & RESTORE

As a result, I pray that you will be impacted with a great sense of urgency concerning the horrible eternal destiny that awaits multitudes of people if they refuse to receive Jesus as their Lord and Savior. Getting a revelation of hell will certainly propel us into soul travail.

A good description or definition of hell is actually found in Webster's Dictionary: the state or place of total and final separation from God and so of eternal misery and suffering, arrived at by those who die unrepentant in grave sin; any place or condition of evil, pain, etc. It's a place of punishment.

Jesus described hell as a place "where their worm does not die, and the fire is not quenched."

Mark 9:44 Where their worm dieth not, and the fire is not quenched.

He also said it was a place of outer darkness and the furnace of fire where there will be wailing, weeping and gnashing of teeth.

Matthew 8:12 But the children of the kingdom shall be cast out into outer darkness: there shall be weeping and gnashing of teeth.

Matthew 13:42 And shall cast them into a furnace of fire: there shall be wailing and gnashing of teeth.

The apostle John, in the book of Revelation, describes hell as a lake of fire burning with brim stone where the beast and the false prophet will end up.

Revelations 19:20 And the beast was taken, and with him the false prophet that wrought miracles before him, with which he deceived them that had received the mark of the beast, and them that worshipped his image. These both were cast alive into a lake of fire burning with brimstone.

At the end of the age the devil will be thrown into this lake of fire (where the beast and the false prophet are also) and they shall be tormented forever.

Revelations 20:10 And the devil that deceived them was cast into the lake of fire and brimstone, where the beast and the false prophet *are,* and shall be tormented day and night for ever and ever.

Also, death and Hades and anyone whose name is not written in the book of life will be thrown into the lake of fire, too.

Revelations 20:14, 15 And death and hell were cast into the lake of fire. This is the second death. And whosoever was not found written in the book of life was cast into the lake of fire.

Hell is translated in the Greek as Gehenna. It is spoken of about thirteen times in the New Testament in this context, and Gehenna actually means valley of Hinnom

(Strong's Concordance #G1067).

This valley, which is a narrow ravine situated on the south end of Jerusalem, has a horrendous history. It was in this area where children died in agony as they were sacrificed to Moloch and Baal.

(2 Kin. 16:3, 23:10, 2 Chr. 28:3, Jer. 7:31).

Because of this wickedness the prophet Jeremiah prophesied that God would bring judgment and destruction on Jerusalem and this valley would be known as the valley of Slaughter.

(Jer. 7:31-32, 19:5-15).

In his religious reforms, Josiah (king of Judah) not only put an end to Israel's idolatrous worship in the high places, he also "defiled" the valley of Hinnom in order to make it unfit for future pagan worship centering on child sacrifice. (2 Kin. 23:1-20)

(This is what hell is. It's even unfit for the pagan worshippers.)

In the time of Jesus the valley of Hinnom was used as a garbage dump refuse, dead bodies of animals and even executed criminals would be incinerated there. The fires would burn continually! Maggots worked in the filth and a thick, foul smoke would blow in the wind, spreading a putrid stench into the atmosphere. All night long wild dogs would howl as they fought over the rotting mess. Jesus used this awful scene as a graphic symbol of hell. (Matt. 5:22, Mark 9:43-45)

All that is unfit for heaven will be poured into hell.

William Booth, the founder of The Salvation Army said (paraphrased): If only every Christian would have visions of hell for thirty minutes to be able to taste of that place. I don't know if I want to see hell for 30 minutes like William Booth suggests! However, I'd like a two minute glimpse of hell because I know my soul would be marked forever.

I'd be ruined (in a good way) with the impact and urgency of the situation for lost humanity more than I ever was before. My mind would shout to me, "Souls are perishing. How awful! I must win souls to Christ because the time is so short!"

It's difficult to think about, but many people will not die happy if they fail to make the most important decision of their lives. That decision is to receive Jesus Christ as their Lord and Savior. Just try to imagine the agony and the anguish for those who do not choose Jesus' gift of salvation.

They'll forfeit their eternal destiny in heaven for never ending torment in hell. Horrible! You know, I believe part of the torment involves memory. By this I mean that those who are in hell will remember each time they rejected Jesus Christ. I believe almost everyone suffers at some point in the "here and now" from bad memories. It's impossible to comprehend the idea of not only being in a place of torment forever, but also having one's memory intact.

If you're like me, you don't want anyone to end up in hell. And that's why it's so important for us to understand that God wants us to co-labor with Him, preparing the soil of people's hearts through soul travail. It's in that place of travail and deep intercession where the spiritual atmosphere is changed so that people are freed up to make a decision for Jesus Christ. Then they're saved. Saved from hell! May God put a powerful desire inside each of us to be moved to snatch people out of the fire?

As for me personally, I want to be able to feel the flames licking at my feet just enough to remind me that I'm saved but even more importantly, that there are multitudes that aren't saved yet. When we know the reality of what's out there HELL FIRE we won't want anyone to feel it or taste it. "God, please give us a revelation about hell!"

Now do you see why it's so important for us to make every effort to go out of our way to reach the lost with the love and the truth of the gospel? When Jesus spoke about the two most important commandments, each one was about love. The first commandment is that we shall love the Lord our God with all our heart, all our soul, all our mind and with all our strength.

The second one is this:

Mark 12:30, 31 And thou shalt love the Lord thy God with all thy heart, and with all thy soul, and with all thy mind, and with all thy strength: this *is* the first commandment. And the second *is* like, *namely* this, Thou shalt love thy neighbour as thyself. There is none other commandment greater than these.

When we really love ourselves God's way, as in those two verses, essentially we confess our sins and we continually check to be sure our soul is right with God. But did you know that we can also love our neighbor the same way that we love ourselves? When we really love the people that God puts in our lives, one of the first things we'll be concerned about is whether or not their souls are right with God. When we're not just concerned about ourselves but we also care about the eternal destiny of our neighbor, this demonstrates "love your neighbor as yourself." You know, parents, if possible, would pay any price required in order to save our child from any devilish plan. If money was demanded, if we could, we'd pay any amount because after all, it's our child's life and soul that's at stake. But are we willing to pay the price so that our neighbor isn't destroyed by the devil?

God wants us to "love our neighbor as our self" just like we would love our own flesh and blood, our own children. He wants us to be able to pay the price required in order to see that people make a decision for Jesus Christ. But in order to pay the price, as I said last week, we need to be "pregnant" with the desire and burden of God's heart that souls be saved.

As always, Jesus Christ is our example. After Jesus went into the cities and villages preaching the gospel of the kingdom and healing the sick, He had an important message for His disciples to hear because He was "pregnant" with His Father's heart. Here's what He said to His disciples, "The harvest truly is plentiful, but the laborers are few.

Matthew 9:37, 38 Then saith he unto his disciples, The harvest truly *is* plenteous, but the labourers *are* few; Pray ye therefore the Lord of the harvest, that he will send forth labourers into his harvest.

He challenged His disciples at this point because He was touched with the heart of His Father for the poor, the needy and the lost. As He looked at the multitude, His heart was moved with compassion. He wanted all of their sicknesses to be healed and He wanted to bring them into a salvation experience. But He needed help to accomplish this mission. When He spoke about the harvest and the laborers being so few, it's like He was making an appeal to His disciples.

If birthing a baby is work, then how much more is the birthing of souls in the spirit? There is labor, there is pain and there is a process that takes place. We cannot expect spiritual babes to be born without experiencing agonizing, fervent prayer. We need to be "wrestlers with God" for souls.

We need to become like Jacob,

Genesis 32:24-30 And Jacob was left alone; and there wrestled a man with him until the breaking of the day. And when he saw that he prevailed not against him, he touched the hollow of his thigh; and the hollow of Jacob's thigh was out of joint, as he wrestled with him. And he said, Let me go, for the day breaketh. And he said, I will not let thee go, except thou bless me. And he said unto him, What *is* thy name? And he said, Jacob. And he said, Thy name shall be called no more Jacob, but Israel: for as a prince hast thou power with God and with men, and hast prevailed. And Jacob asked *him,* and said,

Tell *me,* I pray thee, thy name. And he said, Wherefore *is* it *that* thou dost ask after my name? And he blessed him there. And Jacob called the name of the place Peniel: for I have seen God face to face, and my life is preserved.

Have you ever been so moved to see someone saved that you locked yourself in your room for 24 hours with no food or drink while you prayed and cried out to God. That kind of intercession is desperate! It's work! There has to be that agonizing prayer, that process. God wants to bring us into that intense place of soul travail. He wants to bring forth salvation and bring forth life!

But like I mentioned earlier, we can only do it when we're pregnant and moved by the Holy Spirit. So let's examine four different examples of fervent prayer (by the prophet Joel, the apostle Paul, the prophet Elijah and the apostles). Although each example may not necessarily illustrate specific travail over souls, they certainly model "extreme" prayer. I say we need to become like the prophet Joel! He became pregnant with a burden and he heard from the Lord to consecrate a fast and gather with the priests and the people to pray and cry out to the Lord.

Joel 1:14 Sanctify ye a fast, call a solemn assembly, gather the elders *and* all the inhabitants of the land *into* the house of the LORD your God, and cry unto the LORD,

Joel 2:15 Blow the trumpet in Zion, sanctify a fast, call a solemn assembly:

The key to getting the breakthrough that his nation needed would happen through great travail, deep intercession and fasting.

We've lost that kind of prayer. God is convicting me: "Bill you're going to pray over that situation and you're going to deal with your heart until you get to the place where you're so in touch with the burden that you can really pray. If you're just going to pray out of obligation and do a courtesy prayer, forget it Bill. I'm not going to hear you!"

God wants us to wrestle and lay hold of the situation and birth the answer in the spiritual realm first and pull it out of that invisible realm. Most of the time all we do is touch it or pass by it or scrape up against it. "Ah, it's too much commitment! Ah, it's too much work! Ah, You require too much of me!" And we let go. We need to bring it out of the invisible.

Galatians 4:19 My little children, of whom I travail in birth again until Christ be formed in you,

Paul had already labored and travailed for their spiritual birth and once again he is in labor until Christ is formed in them. He's birthing their godly character through intercession and prayer.

When Paul wrote to the Ephesians, it's evident that his heart attitude was profoundly prayerful. He said,

Ephesians 3:14 For this cause I bow my knees unto the Father of our Lord Jesus Christ,

He was continually in that place of birthing. He knew that realm and he knew how to touch the heart of God and how to bring forth and birth what God desired. We need this attitude, too!

When Elijah the prophet heard from the Lord that He wanted to send rain and break the famine in Israel, he became pregnant with birthing God's plan.

## INCREASE OF REVELATION AND RESTORATION: REVEAL, RECOVER & RESTORE

1 Kings 18:1 And it came to pass *after* many days, that the word of the LORD came to Elijah in the third year, saying, Go, shew thyself unto Ahab; and I will send rain upon the earth.

In his spirit he heard the sound of the abundance of rain before the rain actually came down.

1 Kings 18:41 And Elijah said unto Ahab, Get thee up, eat and drink; for *there is* a sound of abundance of rain.

So he went up to Mount Carmel, got into a birthing position with this head between his knees, and he began to intercede for the rain to come. Next, he sent his servant to go and see if any clouds were on the horizon. Time after time his servant came back without sighting anything. So Elijah kept himself in a birthing position, didn't give up, and he kept on praying. Finally the seventh time his servant saw a cloud as small as a man's hand coming up from the sea.

1 Kings 18:44 And it came to pass at the seventh time, that he said, Behold, there ariseth a little cloud out of the sea, like a man's hand. And he said, Go up, say unto Ahab, Prepare *thy chariot,* and get thee down, that the rain stop thee not.

Even though it was a small cloud, it grew! So Elijah called the rain forth (that God said would come) and it wasn't long before a heavy rain pelted the parched ground! Now that's travail; that's birthing God's purposes in the earth.

We need to sense God's plan in our spirit, too, and then move into that place of relentless intercession. As persecution mounted, some of the apostles were jailed but later they escaped when an angel of the Lord opened the gates of their prison during the night.

Acts 5:17-19 Then the high priest rose up, and all they that were with him, (which is the sect of the Sadducees,) and were filled with indignation, And laid their hands on the apostles, and put them in the common prison. But the angel of the Lord by night opened the prison doors, and brought them forth, and said, It was a time of miracles and conversions! The church was growing and in the middle of all the excitement there arose a legitimate complaint.

Acts 6:1 And in those days, when the number of the disciples was multiplied, there arose a murmuring of the Grecians against the Hebrews, because their widows were neglected in the daily ministration.

The apostles decided not to involve themselves in the problem and so they suggested a remedy.

Acts 6:2, 3 Then the twelve called the multitude of the disciples *unto them,* and said, It is not reason that we should leave the word of God, and serve tables. Wherefore, brethren, look ye out among you seven men of honest report, full of the Holy Ghost and wisdom, whom we may appoint over this business.

Here's the reason why they didn't want to become involved:

Acts 6:4 But we will give ourselves continually to prayer, and to the ministry of the word.

The apostles knew they had to be in that place of prayer, birthing souls into the kingdom of God. Their wise choice to devote themselves to prayer and the ministry of the word helped the word of God to spread to the point that the number of the disciples multiplied greatly in Jerusalem and even many of the priests were obedient to the faith.

The number of disciples went from "multiplying" to "multiplied greatly"

Acts 6:1 And in those days, when the number of the disciples was multiplied, there arose a murmuring of the Grecians against the Hebrews, because their widows were neglected in the daily ministration.

Acts 6:7 And the word of God increased; and the number of the disciples multiplied in Jerusalem greatly; and a great company of the priests were obedient to the faith.

They realized that the key to the continuation of the harvest and the fuel to the revival with mighty signs and wonders were the word of God and prayer. Prayer was first and foremost! They placed such importance on that and we need to come back to that place of prayer for the lost, too.

I want to say that each person who hasn't yet received Jesus as their Lord and Savior is actually blinded by the god of this world and is subject to control by the power of the prince of the air.

Ephesians 2:1, 2 And you *hath he quickened,* who were dead in trespasses and sins; Wherein in time past ye walked according to the course of this world, according to the prince of the power of the air, the spirit that now worketh in the children of disobedience:

In this condition, the demonic realm has a right to try to keep these people blind to the gospel message and to hinder a salvation experience. But all is not lost! We can co-labor with the Holy Spirit to set them free. Help is on the way!

James 5:16 Confess *your* faults one to another, and pray one for another, that ye may be healed. The effectual fervent prayer of a righteous man availeth much.

I want to help you move into labor and travail for lost souls to be saved in a different way than you may have been taught before.

Isaiah 61:1, 2 The Spirit of the Lord GOD *is* upon me; because the LORD hath anointed me to preach good tidings unto the meek; he hath sent me to bind up the brokenhearted, to proclaim liberty to the captives, and the opening of the prison to *them that are* bound; To proclaim the acceptable year of the LORD, and the day of vengeance of our God; to comfort all that mourn;

Based on this scripture, the Spirit of the Lord is upon "us," to set the captives free and to proclaim liberty and freedom to the prisoners. We are anointed to proclaim liberty to the captives and to open the prison doors for those who are bound! God is our source, friend, and Christ lives in us

Colossians 1:27 To whom God would make known what *is* the riches of the glory of this mystery among the Gentiles; which is Christ in you, the hope of glory:

John 1:1 In the beginning was the Word, and the Word was with God, and the Word was God.

When we do our part the Holy Spirit has great freedom to do His work. In fact, this is what it means to co-labor with the Holy Spirit. These verses in Isaiah can be used to inspire our prayers! We can actually transform hopeless looking situations out from under the devil's control. Let's suppose that you're praying for your son Daniel. He's blind and doesn't comprehend the truth and it's like there is a veil over his understanding. So here's how to pray and release him in the spiritual realm so he can actually hear the gospel and be saved. "I loose you Daniel by the power and the anointing of the name of Jesus Christ. The god of this world that is blinding Daniel, remove your veil off of Daniel! I proclaim an opening of the prison for Daniel and freedom. I bind you devil, and I bind your influence so that he can receive the gospel message of the Lord Jesus Christ and be saved!" Don't give up praying like this! Instead of asking God to do it, we are supposed to rise up in the power and authority that Jesus gave us and proclaim liberty and the opening of the prison to those who are bound.

We're supposed to set them free in the spirit realm by the name of Jesus, by the anointing, by speaking their name, and by speaking to the devil and letting him know that you know your authority. Use the Word of the Lord. It's a sword! You have the legal right! "Hey devil, I know what the Word of God says in 2 Corinthians 4, Ephesians 2, Isaiah 61 and Luke 10. Power and authority is given unto me." And you rise up and take that authority and you snatch people out of the fire. Whoever you are praying for will have some kind of visitation by the Holy Spirit (unless their consciences are seared to the point that the Holy Spirit knows there is no hope left for them.

1 Timothy 4:1, 2 Now the Spirit speaketh expressly, that in the latter times some shall depart from the faith, giving heed to seducing spirits, and doctrines of devils; Speaking lies in hypocrisy; having their conscience seared with a hot iron;

Mark 3:29 But he that shall blaspheme against the Holy Ghost hath never forgiveness, but is in danger of eternal damnation:

Not only do we have the power and the right to make decrees and pray violently, but we also have a legal right especially in the area of our household.

Look at what the apostle Paul said to the jailer after an earthquake freed him from prison:

Acts 16:31 And they said, Believe on the Lord Jesus Christ, and thou shalt be saved, and thy house.

Although the jailer didn't appear to be a God fearing man, that didn't stop Paul from decreeing words of life, not only for him, but for his whole household!

How much more then, do blood-bought, born again believers have a weighty legal right to see their household saved. We need a revelation about this! We need to realize that we have great "clout" that activates favor and success when we travail and labor in prayer for our households to be saved.

(Clout means: influence, pull, power or muscle—The American Heritage Dictionary.)

The Bible sites two more faith-inspiring household salvation stories. One is found in Acts 10 concerning Cornelius and his household and the other in Acts 16 concerning Lydia and her household. It's interesting that both Cornelius and Lydia honored God before they and their households were actually saved. However, as I mentioned earlier, the jailer didn't appear to be a God-fearing man.

Acts 16:27-34 And the keeper of the prison awaking out of his sleep, and seeing the prison doors open, he drew out his sword, and would have killed himself, supposing that the prisoners had been fled. But Paul cried with a loud voice, saying, Do thyself no harm: for we are all here. Then he called for a light, and sprang in, and came trembling, and fell down before Paul and Silas, And brought them out, and said, Sirs, what must I do to be saved? And they said, Believe on the Lord Jesus Christ, and thou shalt be saved, and thy house.

And they spake unto him the word of the Lord, and to all that were in his house. And he took them the same hour of the night, and washed *their* stripes; and was baptized, he and all his, straightway. And when he had brought them into his house, he set meat before them, and rejoiced, believing in God with all his house.

He actually feared man and was about to kill himself "supposing that the prisoners had escaped." However, God saw his heart and not only was he saved, so was his whole household! Furthermore, the book of Acts isn't the only book of the Bible where household salvation is mentioned.

Exodus 12:3 Speak ye unto all the congregation of Israel, saying, In the tenth *day* of this month they shall take to them every man a lamb, according to the house of *their* fathers, a lamb for an house:

Many of you will remember that Exodus 12 is the biblical account of the Passover. God instructed the children of Israel to sacrifice an unblemished male lamb and then take its blood and put it on their doorposts and on the lintel (the horizontal crosspiece over their door).

Here's why. Later that night when the angel of death came by, the angel would see the blood and therefore "pass over" that particular household.

Exodus 12:29 And it came to pass, that at midnight the LORD smote all the firstborn in the land of Egypt, from the firstborn of Pharaoh that sat on his throne unto the firstborn of the captive that *was* in the dungeon; and all the firstborn of cattle.

Everyone inside that particular house would live household salvation! On the other hand, any household without the blood-covering suffered the death of their first-born (as a judgment from God). By following God's instructions, the children of Israel demonstrated prophetically the salvation message of the gospel.

I say this because Jesus Christ is the Lamb of God and His blood was shed for our sins. When we receive Jesus Christ as our Lord and Savior, we're receiving His atonement for our sins because His blood atones for our sins and then death has to pass over us. Therefore we don't die and go to hell!

1 Corinthians 15:54, 55 So when this corruptible shall have put on incorruption, and this mortal shall have put on immortality, then shall be brought to pass the saying that is written, Death is swallowed up in victory. O death, where *is* thy sting? O grave, where *is* thy victory?

Deliverance from bondage and sin! We can move in the anointing of God and travail for souls to be saved in our household.

Soul travail can have even wider applications. There are many exciting historical accounts of revivals that happened because people were moved to pray and travail for souls to be saved. I want to share a quote by William Branham, considered by many to be the catalyst of the healing and charismatic revival that began in 1947.

When Jonathan Edwards gave his famous sermon, Sinners in the Hands of an Angry God, the Spirit of God was mightily poured out. God so manifested His holiness and majesty during the preaching of that sermon that the elders threw their arms around the pillars of the church and cried, "Lord, save us. We are slipping down into hell."

# INCREASE OF REVELATION AND RESTORATION:
## REVEAL, RECOVER & RESTORE

(We tend to focus on that great sermon and we think about the power of the Holy Spirit. But what helped to pave the way for such a great move of the Holy Spirit was soul travail! The whole congregation of that church was in fervent prayer all the previous night.) When I look into history and see some of the men and women of God who successfully brought souls into a salvation experience, I am aware of the unsung heroes travailing behind the scenes, in secret, for souls to be saved.

God is calling us back into prayer and back to the secret place. He is calling us into soul travail. Are we willing?

When the Spirit of God falls on us, nothing will stand in the way of our prayers. This is our soul travail and it causes souls to be snatched from the fire! When God's grace comes, the anointing for prayer and supplication comes upon us out of heaven. It's not just us doing the praying apart from the Holy Spirit. Rather, we are co-laboring with the Holy Spirit.

Supplication comes forth through us by the power of the Holy Spirit and we're moved powerfully by the Spirit to pray.

We're pregnant with the desires of God's heart. Today, my hope and prayer is that you are ready to co-labor with the Holy Spirit in passionate soul travail, so that souls will be saved.

# Stirring the Spirit of Revelation

God has been releasing a much greater level of revelation than ever before. In fact He has saved revelations coming now until this time. Through this Chapter, I want to show you how to stir up the spirit of wisdom and revelation that the scripture refers to in Revelation 4. It's time that we, as the church, take back our inheritance our call to see into the spiritual realm and live as supernatural beings living in a physical body. In order to walk into this inheritance, we need to be set free from the fear of deception which plagues so much of the church. When we have a biblical foundation for our lives and we see how naturally God's people have lived in the supernatural realm from the beginning to the end of the Bible, we can rest in the knowledge that such experiences are good gifts from the Father. Yes, we need to lay out some guidelines through practical teaching on the do's and don'ts of experiencing the supernatural and handling revelation that is what I intend to do in this Chapter.

It is my prayer that this Chapter will stir up revelation knowledge in you: word of knowledge, visions, and the whole prophetic realm. Do you want an increase of the prophetic in your life so you can hear God's voice clearer and increasingly experience wonderful encounters with the Holy Spirit? If so, then today is your day for flying higher in the supernatural realm. The first thing you need to understand is that true divine revelation is available in abundance and it's available to you! You need to understand how easy it is to receive revelation so you can grow in faith. God wants you to have great expectations of how much spiritual knowledge we can receive now if we will just learn to receive from Him. My desire is to raise the level of your expectation that God will speak to you and that He will give you supernatural revelation if you open your spirit to Him by faith. We can truly trust Him to bless us with revelation because scripture tells us that if we ask for a good gift He won't give us something harmful God is in the business of giving good things to those who ask Him.

Matthew 7:10, 11 Or if he ask a fish, will he give him a serpent? If ye then, being evil, know how to give good gifts unto your children, how much more shall your Father which is in heaven give good things to them that ask him?

The greatest of those good gifts the Father wants to give us is relationship with Him, which involves communication and hearing His voice. Remember, as believers, we have the Holy Spirit living inside of us. Scripture tells us that the Spirit searches all things, even the deep things of God He searches the mind of Christ. Consequently, because I have the Holy Spirit in me, anywhere I am, at any moment, I have access to the thoughts and the mind of Christ. I can also access the deep things of God through the Spirit in me who brings revelation and searches all things.

When I saw this truth and started to lift my faith and expectation that I could be used in the prophetic and that I could hear God's voice, revelation from heaven began to increase. However, let me point out here that many of you may

# INCREASE OF REVELATION AND RESTORATION:
## REVEAL, RECOVER & RESTORE

have heard God's voice and even prophesied, maybe a little on Sunday or a little song of the Lord here and there you've had the inspiration, the unction and the leading of the Spirit. But that's not the realm I'm talking about; I am talking about the extreme level of the prophetic visitations of angels, trances, visions and visits into the third heaven. I believe God wants to speak in these "extreme" ways as well as through promptings and the still small voice.

When I began to see in scripture how natural these experiences were, I realized that I could also have trances like Peter; that I, like the apostle Paul, could go into paradise; and that I, like Ezekiel, could be taken by the Spirit into visions of God.

I started expecting, not just the prophetic, the still small voice, the little divine thoughts, or the body impressions of other people's pains or sicknesses. My faith started growing for experiencing God in a whole new realm, a realm of supernatural revelation common for those walking in the seer anointing. I started to believe that I could have a seer anointing like Elisha. The bible illustrates that this anointing can be received in prayer consider the story of Elisha praying for his servant, Gehazi, that the eyes of his heart could be opened to see into the second heaven (the realm of demons). So I stretched my faith, to believe for a whole new dimension of the prophetic praying in faith became easy when I realized that revelation is available in abundance through the Holy Spirit inside me. So, anywhere I am, it is as easy as tuning into the Spirit of God within me to receive revelation from heaven.

The Bible says that God's thoughts toward us are precious and as innumerable as the sand of the sea.

Psalms 139:17, 18 How precious also are thy thoughts unto me, O God! how great is the sum of them! *If* I should count them, they are more in number than the sand: when I awake, I am still with thee.

God doesn't just have one thought toward us the Bible tells us His thoughts are countless. I believe that God wants to share those thoughts with us because, by His Spirit, He has given us the mind of Christ. Sometimes revelation from God is as easy as asking for just one thought that's all it takes to move in the prophetic.

Revelations 4:1 After this I looked, and, behold, a door *was* opened in heaven: and the first voice which I heard *was* as it were of a trumpet talking with me; which said, Come up hither, and I will shew thee things which must be hereafter.

So if heaven is going to touch earth with miracles, healings, signs, wonders, visions and revelation, heaven must be opened up for us. It was when heaven opened that John the apostle began to receive revelation.

Revelations 19:11 And I saw heaven opened, and behold a white horse; and he that sat upon him *was* called Faithful and True, and in righteousness he doth judge and make war.

As the church, we need to pray for an open heaven because that's what causes the prophetic to be released. In Revelation 4:1 a door is standing open in heaven and there comes an invitation: "Come up here, and I will show you things which must take place after this." I believe that John received revelation because that heavenly door never closed. And that door is still standing open in heaven today. As in Jacob's vision of the ladder going into heaven with the angels ascending and descending, those heavenly beings are still going into heaven and coming out with revelation from God. Jacob's ladder, I believe, is still available to us today, to enable us to come into the spirit just like John, we can say, "immediately, I was in the spirit."

By faith we need to raise our expectation levels of how much we believe we can have now. I believe there is a door standing open in heaven and that we are invited to "Come up here!" When I saw that this same invitation was for me, I began to say, "Holy Spirit come, I'm climbing up that ladder. I'm going into the heavens; I'm getting revelation and bringing it out into the earth." Many of us don't experience this realm and dimension of the prophetic because we never put our faith out there for it. We might reach for a little prophecy but we never reach for angels or trances.

Revelations 4:6 And before the throne *there was* a sea of glass like unto crystal: and in the midst of the throne, and round about the throne, *were* four beasts full of eyes before and behind.

Have you ever wondered about the significance of the creatures full of eyes and of the crystal sea? Nothing can be hidden. Because He is the Alpha and Omega, He knows the Beginning and the End.

The vision gave me a prophetic picture of God's all seeing and all knowing ability from the beginning until the end of time. He knows the thoughts and hearts of every man and every woman who has ever lived.

The Lord told me He was taking His church deeper in revelation, for the knowledge of the glory of the Lord will cover the earth as the water covers the sea. That knowledge went on further than my eyes could see.

Then the Lord showed me that the eyes represented His all-knowing, all-seeing ability. Ezekiel 10 also refers to these eyes. However, this passage describes cherubim, full of eyes, moving with God's glory. Whenever the glory of the Lord moved with the Ark of the Covenant, the cherubim would move in the same direction. The eyes (the revelation) could be found everywhere the glory presence of the Lord went. We need to understand that heaven is full of revelation and that revelation is available to us, His children. When you come into God's presence, it's like coming into the sea of glass or that place in heaven where all the eyes are.

God wants to release that revelation knowledge to you today.

Besides the crystal sea and the eyes, scripture uses another symbol in,

1 Samuel 14:29 Then said Jonathan, My father hath troubled the land: see, I pray you, how mine eyes have been enlightened, because I tasted a little of this honey.

I believe honey, here and throughout scripture is a prophetic picture of revelation. When Jonathan took that honey and he tasted it, it brightened his countenance, quickened his understanding and made him sharp. That is what happens when you get into revelation it makes you quick and sharp. This is often the case for prophetic people. Revelation supernaturally transforms your imagination and understanding. People ask how you can even be able to write thirteen books in three to four months. How does that happen?

Well, I believe that being in the anointing and being exposed to the spirit of wisdom and revelation quickens your understanding. Revelation actually does something to your physical body; it actually does something to your mind. Perhaps you're saying today, "That is what I need. Give me a little of that spirit of wisdom and revelation."

We need to recognize that revelation comes from the Holy Ghost. Remember Jesus' words to Peter after he said that Jesus was the Son of God: "Flesh and blood has not revealed this to you but my Father who is in heaven." Yes, the Father has sent the Holy Spirit to give us revelation He lives inside each born-again believer. Also, it's important to know that revelation can be connected to a geographic place. I have been to regions of the earth where I experienced heightened revelation just because of where I was geographically I was in a place under a greater open heaven.

Genesis 28:10 And Jacob went out from Beersheba, and went toward Haran.

Remember he went to a "certain place."

Jacob slept there that night because the sun had set. Verse 12 tells us that he dreamed in that same place. The dream was connected to the place.

Atmosphere has everything to do with revelation. In scripture, when the minstrel played, the hand of the Lord came. God's throne on earth begins to be established when we worship. The seraphim angels in Revelation 4 worship 24 hours a day, saying, "Holy, Holy, Holy, Lord God Almighty, who was and is and is to come!" In that atmosphere of worship, we become transparent before God and He gives us eyes to see into the spirit realm. As we worship, God's glory presence becomes tangible and the creatures that cover and protect the cherubim and seraphim begin to be activated. As we worship together, God begins to change the atmosphere so that revelation can be released. When the minstrel plays, the hand of the Lord comes.

So, I believe that there are atmospheres connected to geographical locations that make it easier for us to ascend into the heavens and return to earth with revelation. As I continue to teach on the spirit of wisdom and revelation, I believe God wants to give you a powerful impartation from heaven. As you open your spirit right now, you can begin to receive down loads from the spirit. So you go ahead and have visions, trances, dreams or go to heaven any time that you want to. I expect you to see.

Ephesians 1:17 That the God of our Lord Jesus Christ, the Father of glory, may give unto you the spirit of wisdom and revelation in the knowledge of him:

As this scripture shows us, wisdom and revelation is always connected to the knowledge of Him. This "knowledge of Him" is not knowledge about God. It's not the knowledge of scripture. It's not the knowledge of who God is and what He does. It's not the knowledge of theology and principles.

This passage speaks of knowing Him through experience and intimacy because we have taken the time to be in His presence and we've taken the time to know Him, His ways, His heart and His character. God is calling us to receive the knowledge that only comes through experience because we have been at his feet. The more we grow in the knowledge of Him, the more the spirit of wisdom and revelation will increase in our life.

God wants to give us the ministry of Jesus, which is the ministry of revelation.

Isaiah 11:2 And the spirit of the LORD shall rest upon him, the spirit of wisdom and understanding, the spirit of counsel and might, the spirit of knowledge and of the fear of the LORD;

These aspects of God's nature all go together. The Spirit of the Lord rests on Jesus' wisdom and understanding as well as counsel which brings might and revelation which brings power!

Jesus said He only did those things He saw His Father doing.

So the revelation what He saw the Father doing by vision He went and did in the earth? This combination of revelation, faith and obedience is what brought the power. I believe the passage in Isaiah shows us that counsel brings might these two spirits and natures of the Lord work together. Some of you don't have more might in your life because you don't have counsel in your life, because you're not tapping into God's heart and mind by stirring up the spirit of wisdom and revelation. Or perhaps you just haven't had the faith and expectation that this kind of prophetic is for you. You may have thought it was for the prophet but not for you. However, God wants powerful revelation from heaven to become a common and everyday release in the body of Christ. We need to take the spookiness out of it trances, dreams and heavenly visitations need to become natural and common in the body of Christ because that is what the ministry of Jesus was. The ministry of Jesus was wisdom, understanding, counsel, might, knowledge and the fear of the Lord.

Ephesians 1:17, 18 That the God of our Lord Jesus Christ, the Father of glory, may give unto you the spirit of wisdom and revelation in the knowledge of him: The eyes of your understanding being enlightened; that ye may know what is the hope of his calling, and what the riches of the glory of his inheritance in the saints,

That is what revelation does it brings a revelation of God's call and a sense of His purpose and destiny for your life. Without revelation we don't have that fire in our spirit, that desire, that love of Christ that constrains us or that fire that motivates moves and compels us. We need that passion inside us that says, this is who I am and this is what I am going to do. This passion only comes out of revelation.

God also wants the eyes of our heart to be open so we can also understand what are "the riches of the glory of His inheritance in the saints, and what is the exceeding greatness of His power toward us who believe, according to the working of His mighty power which He worked in Christ when He raised Him from the Dead." Yes, the spirit of wisdom and revelation, as well as having the eyes of our heart enlightened, brings us into the manifestation of God's power. Without the revelation, we won't have a manifestation of Gods power because revelation is connected to the power of God, to miracles, signs and wonders. Revelation is always connected to raising the dead.

So where is this power? Is it in your life? Where is the manifestation of the exceeding greatness of His power? Somewhere along the line, the penny hasn't dropped. Somewhere along the line, we really haven't had revelation; we've only had knowledge. However, when the revelation happens, the manifestation happens and the demonstration happens. That is how Elijah operated.

# INCREASE OF REVELATION AND RESTORATION:
## REVEAL, RECOVER & RESTORE

You know what revelation is? The word revelation means to reveal and disclose it is the secrets of the Lord. Revelation means appearing; it speaks of lightning; it means "the coming" and "the manifestation." Manifestation brings the revelation into the natural realm. We desperately need to have an increase of the spirit of wisdom and revelation. You know what wisdom is. Wisdom involves correct delivery and it means to rightly divide knowledge. When we receive God's wisdom, we know when and how to present our revelation to others in Christ's body. As the Lord discloses the secrets of His heart to us faith rises in our hearts to see these spiritual things become a natural reality. If we don't have a revelation of the exceeding greatness of His power, we won't have the manifestation of the exceeding greatness of His power.

So how do we cultivate the lifestyle of receiving wisdom and revelation?

I am going to share with you ways that you can stir up, and practically increase, the spirit of wisdom and revelation in your life.

2 Peter 1:2, 3 Grace and peace be multiplied unto you through the knowledge of God, and of Jesus our Lord, According as his divine power hath given unto us all things that *pertain* unto life and godliness, through the knowledge of him that hath called us to glory and virtue:

**Intimacy:** Notice that the first thing about revelation is that it is always connected to intimate knowledge of Him. According to verse three, God has given us his divine power for everything pertaining to life, to divine power and to activating the provision of everything that we need to live a life of godliness it's all connected to the intimate knowledge of Him.

All these treasures come from acquaintance with Him through prayer, intimacy, worship, and sitting at His feet and being in His presence. As a result, the manifestation of His divine power comes automatically to give us everything we need to be as godly as God has called us to be. God has already made the provision; we just receive it through growing in intimate knowledge of Him.

Now, look at verse two: "Grace and peace be multiplied to you." How about you? Would you like the multiplication of grace and peace in your life? Again we see these blessings automatically poured into our lives in intimacy with Jesus. This grace is the divine influence or the evidence of God on the heart as well as the gift, favor and benefits of God. Wouldn't you like more of the favor of God, His divine benefits and supernatural influence in your life? When that grace is multiplied, God's power is manifested on your life as well. It automatically takes place in intimacy isn't that awesome!

Peace is also a fruit of intimacy. The word peace means quietness, rest, prosperity and wholeness. How would you like the multiplication of this great peace that passes all understanding? More Lord! As these wonderful blessings of grace and peace come on our lives in intimacy, we have more prosperity, quietness, rest, health and wholeness.

The Father wants to give us everything we need for an abundant, godly life.

2 Peter 1:4 Whereby are given unto us exceeding great and precious promises: that by these ye might be partakers of the divine nature, having escaped the corruption that is in the world through lust.

Verse four tells us that we can become a partaker of the divine nature of God. We partake through the exceeding great and precious promises that have opened the door to fellowship, communion, partnership and association with God's divine nature, the very substance and character of who God and who Christ is. The character of God is locked up in the spirit of wisdom and in the spirit of revelation.

As we grow in revelation of the exceeding great and precious promises of God's word, an impartation of the divine nature of God comes automatically. When we flow in the prophetic anointing, the very divine nature, character, spirit and personality of Christ is imparted to us in intimacy through revelation.

We will find people saying to us, "Wow, you do have more benefits; you do have more favor and you do have more power in your life. Why are you so blessed? You have more wholeness, more prosperity, more shalom, more quietness and more rest in your life." Then we can tell them that it's all connected to being intimately connected with Him. We become more like Him just because we are having revelation of the exceeding great and precious promises of God's word!

*Meditation*: The second thing that stirs up wisdom and revelation in our life is receiving the rhema promise of God through meditation. In 2 Peter 1:19, we can learn more about how to partake of the exceeding great and precious promise: "And so we have the prophetic word confirmed which you do well to heed as a light that shines in a dark place until the day dawns and the morning star rises in your heart." This scripture refers to the prophetic word, the rhema word or the word the

Father speaks personally to our hearts. God's word is like a light that shines in a dark place.

That's how revelation starts God's word shines brightly in dark places in us till the day dawns and the morning star rises in our heart.

So how do we convert that shining inner word into transforming revelation through meditation? Here's how the Lord has taught me to meditate on Scripture. I take God's word or promise and begin to read over it, allowing that light to shine in my heart. As I continue to meditate on the scripture and confess it, pray it, read it, think about it and contemplate day and night, it comes as a light within my heart. And through that process of meditation upon that word, it begins to rise and fill my heart; it begins to rise as the sun at the dawning of a new day. God's rhema, prophetic spoken word to us is always like a light shining in the dark. But as we begin to understand the light of God's word, His word is a lamp to our feet. This is how you partake of the exceeding greatness of His precious promises.

Meditation and revelation are interconnected meditation brings revelation and revelation brings the manifestation of what has been revealed. When we first see or hear the word, it's really not revealed because it is only a light that shines in our heart. However, when we meditate on it and when we pray it, revelation comes and begins working to bring the manifestation and the experience. So why don't we often have the manifestation of what we know? Because we really haven't meditated on those words from the Lord till we received that blazing revelation inside that would release the manifestation of the promise. We need to read and speak out those scriptures and promises over and over again. We've got to say that scripture repeatedly and meditate on a single verse for thirty minutes or more. Then WHAM! It will open up like the drawing of a dark curtain and the Son's light will come on!

***Godly Character*:** The third key to stirring up wisdom and revelation is godly character the passage in 2 Peter continues to provide a blue print for us.

2 Peter 1:5-9 And beside this, giving all diligence, add to your faith virtue; and to virtue knowledge; And to knowledge temperance; and to temperance patience; and to patience godliness; And to godliness brotherly kindness; and to brotherly kindness charity. For if these things be in you, and abound, they make *you that ye shall* neither *be* barren nor unfruitful in the knowledge of our Lord Jesus Christ. But he that lacketh these things is blind, and cannot see afar off, and hath forgotten that he was purged from his old sins.

There is a connection between partaking of the divine nature and character. We begin to long to be more like Jesus: "Lord, I want to be like you. Let me behold you, for I can only become like the one I see. I know I can't really become who you want me to be until I've been in your presence because I become what I see." So as we begin to behold the glory of the Only Begotten Son, as we begin to fix and turn our eyes upon Jesus, as we begin to gaze upon His face and as we begin to spend time in His presence, His character and very nature begins to be forged in us.

Godly character continues to grow as we yield ourselves to the Holy Spirit's cleansing process and as we submit to the discipline of the Father. Our hearts need to cry out for the Spirit of God to change us.

As we love who God is and love His character being worked in us, we are saying: "Holy Spirit help me. I can't do it without you, because I only become what I see. So as I see you, there is a transference that takes place by the Spirit of God to transform us from glory to glory." When our heart cries out like that, the Spirit brings us into an increase of the Spirit of wisdom and revelation because the Bible says that if these things are yours and abound in us, we will not be barren or unfruitful.

Some of you are barren and unfruitful in revelation in your life because of character. On the other hand, some of you are barren and unfruitful in your life because you have an empty well. You can't have revelation if the well is empty, if you haven't been meditating on God's word day and night.

Only as you meditate, and live in intimacy, will you partake of the exceeding great and precious promises as well as His divine nature and character! When you don't partake of God's nature, then you are not fruitful in revelation and you are short-sighted or even blind.

We can't become who God wants us to be without partaking of Him, without the grace, without the divine influence. And the divine influence doesn't happen if we are not in the knowledge of Him. If we are not intimately connected to Him, there isn't the process of the multiplication of the grace, peace and divine influence on our lives to become who He wants us to be. Out of that divine influence, comes everything pertaining to life. Life! God's blessing begins to be poured out on our finances, family, business and physical health. See the whole process is woven together. God has put His divine nature in the prophetic word. In that word releases character growth. A passion to grow in Christ-like character is vitally connected to growing in wisdom and revelation.

Take time to meditate on the first eight verses of 2 Peter chapter 1 until you get the wonderful revelation in this passage.

***Waiting for God's Counsel***: This is the fourth key to stirring up the spirit of wisdom. Psalms 106:13 shows us that receiving revelation is closely connected to waiting for counsel: "They soon forgot His works. They did not wait for His counsel." Verse 15 shows us the consequences of their neglect: "He gave them over to their requests and He sent leanness into their soul." He put a wasting disease in their soul when this happens, as in 1 Samuel 3:1, the word of the Lord becomes rare and visions are infrequent. Are you in a place where the word of the Lord is rare in your life? Are you in a place where visions are infrequent and you're lacking prophetic vision? Perhaps you're saying, "I want an increase. I want to be able to hear the voice of God's Spirit. I want to experience a greater reality of the supernatural. I want daily encounters with God. God please take back the veil and open the eyes of my heart. Please give me an increase of the spirit of wisdom and revelation."

The increase of revelation comes as we wait for His counsel. Revelation was rare to the people of Israel because they weren't taking time to wait in His presence expecting to hear from Him. We need to come to Him saying, "Here I am Lord, an hour before the service tonight, to get counsel of what you want me to do before I do it." Jesus wants us to only do those things that we see the Father doing He doesn't want us doing things just because of traditions or because of man's ideas. I believe Jesus saw what the Father was doing in the place of waiting He would get up a long while before day to pray and

He would wait on the mountain all night. That's where he would get the open vision to see what the Father did so He could go out and do it that day. Jesus received that counsel and revelation because He often withdrew into the wilderness and prayed. And it wasn't just about praying. I believe He had times when He sat at the Father's feet, like Mary sat at His feet, and He didn't say anything. He just looked up at the face of God waiting, waiting, waiting, waiting, and waiting.

Some of you don't wait. I got the word of knowledge flowing in my life waiting on God and being faithful with what He gave me. The more I waited, the more God gave me details about what was wrong with people's bodies. I would take the time on a daily basis, not to pray, but to lie on the carpet, be in His presence, and wait. "What do you want to do tonight Father?" And the next day, "What do you want to do tonight Father?" Pastors often start that way and then they get busy. I wait, at times 1-3 hours a day, everyday in silence for a revelation and for visions.

There was a time in my life when God sovereignly visited me for months, hours a day all I did was lie on the floor and wait for counsel, for wisdom and for revelation. I would just lie in His presence and wait until I would see. As I faithfully did that on a daily basis, God increased the spirit of wisdom and revelation in my life. I'm not talking about being in the word or being in prayer I'm talking about the place in God's presence where you don't do anything but wait.

As we learn to wait on the Lord, the wasting disease and leanness of soul is replaced with; revelation, fruitfulness, favor and financial prosperity. As we spend time waiting before the

# INCREASE OF REVELATION AND RESTORATION: REVEAL, RECOVER & RESTORE

Lord, He opens up the television screen in heaven for us to see what the Father is doing.

***Sanctified Imagination***: If we want to see in the spirit, we must use the powerful key of sanctified imagination to unlock visions and dreams. What do you think about when preachers say, "I saw in the spirit?" Often, we automatically think they saw with their natural eyes. I have helped bring so many people into the heavenly realm by teaching them to look with their spiritual eye and to stop asking, "Where is it? Where is the angel? Where? I don't see him where?" We have to begin to see with our "third eye" the eye on the inside, in our imagination. I showed you this eye in Ephesians 1 it is called the "eyes of your understanding." You don't see spiritual things with natural eyes; you see them with the eyes of your heart, your spiritual eyes! I believe that 90 percent or more of all visions and revelations happen in the eye of our hearts, in our imagination.

Think of how we daydream. That's where visions happen in that same realm, the place of the daydream. However, in this case, God initiates the daydreams. Here's how sanctified daydreaming happens. You're not thinking about anything you're just waiting on the Lord, asking the Holy Spirit to come when God initiates a prophetic daydream. There is such a connection between our thoughts and God's thoughts. That's why we need to sanctify the imagination. So we need to understand that we aren't to look with these eyes, we are to look on the inside.

When people are looking at the screen of our imagination, sometimes I hear them say: "Wait a minute! I think I just saw something. But maybe it was just me, or maybe it was God, or maybe I am just thinking that." Well, so what! Let me ask you a question. If it's not direction and it's not going to alter your life or anybody else's, what is the problem? What if it was really just you thinking that?

My question to you is: "How did that picture make you feel?" If your response is, Man, I felt so close to Him. I felt His love and I could feel the wind blowing on me... then I say, "There it is" that's enough evidence that your vision was from God! Quit trying to analyze it! If you saw yourself with Jesus and it made you cry and it made you feel close to God, that's good enough.

We've got to get over worrying about thinking things up ourselves. If it's not altering anyone's life and we are not dealing with dates, mates or life-altering direction (which you need confirmed in the mouths of two or more witnesses) then we need to stop worrying. But if you're lying on the carpet saying, "Holy Spirit come and sanctify my imagination; I want to be with Jesus in the spirit" and you suddenly go into some kind of prophetic daydream, you just could be having a heavenly experience. You know how I know that? Remember, even Paul the Apostle, when he had his experience in paradise, as grand as it was, said, "Whether in the body... or whether out of the body I do not know."

So even Paul wasn't sure whether he actually physically traveled or whether he was just in paradise in spirit. Paul didn't know, so don't you worry about figuring out all your experiences. However, I will tell you this although sometimes I may have been having a spiritual experience in my imagination, I've often found that others in the same room as me are having the same experience. I may shout out: "I'm in the garden!" or "I'm in the basement!" and they'll shout back, "I'm there too!" When a group of people are all having the same prophetic experience at the same time, you know it must be from God. The more we learn to sanctify the imagination, the more we will experience revelation from the Lord.

***You've got to seek wisdom***: God talks about wisdom and revelation using the personal pronoun "her". To get wisdom, you've got to seek, love and honor her. You've got to promote her. You've got to want her and make yourself available for her. I pursue wisdom on a daily basis. When I got saved I prayed everyday for the Spirit of wisdom. Everyday I spent hours looking for revelation; it became a part of me because it's a part of Jesus.

Let's learn more about this highly-prized wisdom:

Proverbs 2:1-7 My son, if thou wilt receive my words, and hide my commandments with thee; So that thou incline thine ear unto wisdom, *and* apply thine heart to understanding; Yea, if thou criest after knowledge, *and* liftest up thy voice for understanding; If thou seekest her as silver, and searchest for her as *for* hid treasures; Then shalt thou understand the fear of the LORD, and find the knowledge of God. For the LORD giveth wisdom: out of his mouth *cometh* knowledge and understanding. He layeth up sound wisdom for the righteous: *he is* a buckler to them that walk uprightly.

The Lord wants us lift our voice and cry out for understanding. He wants us to "seek her as silver, and search for her as for hidden treasures" then we will "understand the fear of the Lord, and find the knowledge of God." For the Lord gives wisdom, knowledge and understanding to the upright. To the wise King Solomon's counsel about wisdom.

Proverbs 4:5 Get wisdom, get understanding: forget *it* not; neither decline from the words of my mouth.

Do you want an increase of the spirit of wisdom and revelation? Let's begin to follow Solomon's instructions and begin to prayerfully seek for these treasures.

# INCREASE OF REVELATION AND RESTORATION: REVEAL, RECOVER & RESTORE 101

# A New Restoration Movement

God is not just restoring but He is causing this to be turned into a movement. It is time to release this prophetic Chapter. We are about to see a movement across the world of restoration.

I want to invite you to join with me so that, we can nourish ourselves on the Word of God together, as we read a portion from the Apostle Paul's letter to the Ephesian church.

Ephesians 3:14-21 For this cause I bow my knees unto the Father of our Lord Jesus Christ, Of whom the whole family in heaven and earth is named, That he would grant you, according to the riches of his glory, to be strengthened with might by his Spirit in the inner man; That Christ may dwell in your hearts by faith; that ye, being rooted and grounded in love, May be able to comprehend with all saints what *is* the breadth, and length, and depth, and height; And to know the love of Christ, which passeth knowledge, that ye might be filled with all the fulness of God. Now unto him that is able to do exceeding abundantly above all that we ask or think, according to the power that worketh in us, Unto him *be* glory in the church by Christ Jesus throughout all ages, world without end. Amen.

The Lord is ultimately and intimately acquainted with you.

Hebrews 13:5 *Let your* conversation *be* without covetousness; *and be* content with such things as ye have: for he hath said, I will never leave thee, nor forsake thee.

He wants you to know that at all times, especially in the dark times, He is with you and He is the Great Restorer. Listen to what God said through the prophet Joel:

Joel 2:25 And I will restore to you the years that the locust hath eaten, the cankerworm, and the caterpiller, and the palmerworm, my great army which I sent among you.

God loves to restore what has been devoured in our lives. That's His specialty.

Joel records God's message of hope:

Joel 2:21 Fear not, O land; be glad and rejoice: for the LORD will do great things.

God talks about the abundance emphasizing the process of renewal and the release of the latter rain and the spring rain.

Joel 2:23 Be glad then, ye children of Zion, and rejoice in the LORD your God: for he hath given you the former rain moderately, and he will cause to come down for you the rain, the former rain, and the latter rain in the first *month*.

There would be harvest and fruitfulness again.

Joel 2:22 Be not afraid, ye beasts of the field: for the pastures of the wilderness do spring, for the tree beareth her fruit, the fig tree and the vine do yield their strength.

The vats would overflow with new wine.

Joel 2:24 And the floors shall be full of wheat, and the fats shall overflow with wine and oil.

He says, "I am not just going to fill your vats again, your vats are going to overflow! Your barn walls are going to bust

# INCREASE OF REVELATION AND RESTORATION: REVEAL, RECOVER & RESTORE

down!" That's what God does. Biblically; that's what restoration looks like.

Restore in Strong's Exhaustive Concordance of the Bible is: #7999 Hebrew: shalam . . . make amends, (make an) end, finish, full, give again, make good, (re-) pay (again), (make) (to) (be at) peace proper (-ous), recompense, render, require, make restitution, restore, reward, surely.

I've come to realize that when God restores, He brings an increase! When God restores, He multiplies! There is something about the "restoring nature" of God. In the process of restoration God brings the object of restoration back in a better way than was its former state AND He increases it and multiplies it. He always likes to add more!

Look at Job. When God restored Job, He gave unto Job double portion. That's just the nature of God.

Job 42:10 And the LORD turned the captivity of Job, when he prayed for his friends: also the LORD gave Job twice as much as he had before.

In the Bible we see that if harm came to someone or something was stolen, that God would command that the return be greater than what was plundered or robbed.

The odd time the return would be "one for one," but almost every single time the return was ordered to be more than that a double blessing, or four or five times greater (Ex. 22:1; 22:4; Lev. 6:5, 22:14).

And it didn't stop at that point! There was a "seven fold" principle in connection with restoration (and vengeance) as well.

Proverbs 6:31 But *if* he be found, he shall restore sevenfold; he shall give all the substance of his house.

Today, I believe that God ordains it like this in the spirit. When the thief steals he must give back sevenfold. When the devil comes to kill, steal and destroy, God has set forever in eternity that you must get back sevenfold. And God will restore you in a better way than you were at first and then He will increase and multiply what was stolen. That's our God because God is good. We need this revelation.

For instance, when God wants to restore your anointing, it honors Him that you make a declaration like this: "He wants to give me a double portion of anointing!" When God restores, you are going to have double joy, everlasting joy, a double portion! He is going to bless you with an increase and command the thief to give back sevenfold.

If your marriage needs to be restored then stir up your faith and ask: "My God, please, I want You to restore my marriage and I want it to be better than it was in the first place. I want there to be double the intimacy." Get aggressive. Don't just settle for an "okay, restore my marriage" attitude. "Restore my marriage and give it to me double!" "Restore my finances and give it to me double!" "Restore my anointing and give it to me double!" We can ask God because of the nature of the restoration process of the Holy Ghost.

He increases and He multiplies. For instance, when God heals my body, when God restores my body, I'm not just going to be healthy, I am going to have divine health. And then I'm going to minister healing to the sick because I am getting a healing anointing in the process.

That's restoration!

Mark 10:29, 30 And Jesus answered and said, Verily I say unto you, There is no man that hath left house, or brethren, or

## INCREASE OF REVELATION AND RESTORATION: REVEAL, RECOVER & RESTORE

sisters, or father, or mother, or wife, or children, or lands, for my sake, and the gospel's, But he shall receive an hundredfold now in this time, houses, and brethren, and sisters, and mothers, and children, and lands, with persecutions; and in the world to come eternal life.

The Lord does abundantly above what you can ask. He does abundantly above what you can think. We need to have a bigger vision! When we stand in faith and believe that God is hugely enthusiastic about wanting to bring restoration into our lives, we truly honor Him.

God wants you to know that He is extremely interested in accomplishing personal restoration in your life. His desire is that when you experience the blessing of personal restoration (and you will, so have faith), that yes, you will be blessed, but even more, that you will draw closer and closer into His heart. His biggest purpose for restoration is intimacy with you.

Do you realize that without you, without your love and friendship, God is grieved? You know, restoration is something supernatural. After Jesus Christ died on the cross for you and me and we received Him as our Lord and Savior, He restored each one of us into personal relationship and fellowship with Him by taking our sins upon Himself and drawing us into His heart. It's like we are restored in such a way that the experience that Adam and Eve had with God when He walked with them in the cool of the garden is also our experience to enjoy. His presence and His glory were there in the garden. The secret place of His presence is the "garden." Such restoration redeems and it transcends time, space and eternity. And this blessing is available for us today. What an important revelation to have. Yet, the choice is ours.

We can actually choose to stand in faith believing that God wants to restore to us the same kind of special intimacy that He enjoyed with Adam and Eve in the Garden of Eden. I don't believe that we have to wait for the day when we die and go to heaven to enjoy such fellowship with God.

Luke 17:21 Neither shall they say, Lo here! or, lo there! for, behold, the kingdom of God is within you.

From what I see in my Bible, heaven for me began the day that I received eternal life. That is heaven. We are the bride of Christ whether we stand before God individually as His child, or collectively as the body of Christ. I want us to be an excited bride, anticipating the union, the oneness and the intimacy that is reserved for us to take pleasure in, in Christ, with God. He desires to speak to us plainly as a friend speaks to a friend.

To desire the presence of God above all else, and in a much greater way than our common thinking dictates this brings God such great delight! Let's not let religion, man's tradition, or whatever denomination you were raised in, set limits for what you can or cannot receive from the hand of the Lord. There remains a rest in Him. Unbelief has kept us from walking in the full inheritance of everything that we can have in the spirit. I want you to get hungry for God; be more focused on being hungry for the manifestation of the glory of God, union and intimacy.

God opened the garden again! He said to come boldly before the throne. He ripped open the veil.

Hebrews 4:16 Let us therefore come boldly unto the throne of grace, that we may obtain mercy, and find grace to help in time of need.

## INCREASE OF REVELATION AND RESTORATION: REVEAL, RECOVER & RESTORE

Luke 23:45 And the sun was darkened, and the veil of the temple was rent in the midst.

Hebrews 10:19, 20 Having therefore, brethren, boldness to enter into the holiest by the blood of Jesus, By a new and living way, which he hath consecrated for us, through the veil, that is to say, his flesh;

Read about the Garden of Eden and say, "That's mine! There is nothing but me keeping me from that place! Because of the blood of the Lamb, I can enter." Adam and Eve lost access to the garden because of their sin.

Jesus has set us free from the law of sin and death by His shed blood and we aren't blocked from the place of intimacy with God in the garden anymore.

Today, God is going to restore hope to you. So why not prepare your heart right now for what God wants to do in your life.

God is not going to disappoint you and He wants your heart to embrace hope once again the restoration of hope. Let such knowledge become a healing balm to your heart while you reflect on Paul's encouraging message to the Romans.

"Therefore, having been justified by faith, we have peace with God through our Lord Jesus Christ, through whom also we have access by faith into this grace in which we stand, and rejoice in hope of the glory of God. And not only that, but we also glory in tribulations, knowing that tribulation produces perseverance; and perseverance, character; and character, hope. Now hope does not disappoint, because the love of God has been poured out in our hearts by the Holy Spirit who was given to us"

Romans 5:1-5 Therefore being justified by faith, we have peace with God through our Lord Jesus Christ: By whom also we have access by faith into this grace wherein we stand, and rejoice in hope of the glory of God. And not only *so,* but we glory in tribulations also: knowing that tribulation worketh patience; And patience, experience; and experience, hope: And hope maketh not ashamed; because the love of God is shed abroad in our hearts by the Holy Ghost which is given unto us.

Our Father in heaven is good and He is the Great Restorer. You should have high hopes about that and believe it, no matter what happens. Believe that God not only wants to restore what has been robbed and plundered in your life and in other people's lives, but He also wants to add blessings to that which is restored.

Proverbs 10:6 Blessings *are* upon the **head of the just**: but violence covereth the mouth of the wicked.

That's your head!

When God restores and blesses; He wants you to see His intervention as evidence of His love for you in a personal way. So let's remember that one important aspect about restoration is that you would draw closer and closer into God's heart of love. His biggest purpose for restoration is intimacy with you. He wants an intimate relationship with you. Wow!

So, restoration is like a two-edged sword. One sharp edge reveals our own personal restoration victories and the other edge cuts off the plans of the enemy over other people's lives. What a double blessing!

But we need to remember that in the process of restoration there is always a divine test. Before Joseph's freedom was restored and he took the throne in Egypt (second only to

Pharaoh), he was taken into a great God-ordained time of testing.

Psalms 105:19 Until the time that his word came: the word of the LORD tried him.

Joseph had the prophetic word of the Lord but until it actually came to pass, this word tested him. Likewise, many of you have the prophetic word of the Lord concerning areas of restoration coming upon your lives; however, today, the fulfillment has not manifested, it's still on its way. Stand your ground in the time of testing, the time of waiting. God will surely come and bring restoration exactly at the perfect moment.

I believe that God is going to stir up the gifts of the Spirit in your life. God is going to restore your anointing. For some of you He is going to restore your vision and your purpose. For some of you, God is going to restore your marriage. Some of you will experience God restoring your finances and giving you jubilee and supernatural cancellation of your debt. Say, "God, I want you to restore my soul. Anoint my head with fresh oil." The anointing is going to restore your soul, your mind, your will, and your emotions.

Proverbs 10:22 The blessing of the LORD, it maketh rich, and he addeth no sorrow with it.

Hallelujah! Your restoration looks like a two-edged sword! You won't only receive the blessing of restoration; you will be a minister of restoration!

Walking in the ministry of restoration is like being a minister filled with a message of hope that transforms what was into the reality of what God desires.

Look at what God says through Isaiah (the prophet).

Isaiah 61:4 And they shall build the old wastes, they shall raise up the former desolations, and they shall repair the waste cities, the desolations of many generations.

It's the rebuilding, the raising up and the repairing of ruins and ruined cities and the desolations of many generations. It's a transformation process into the reality of what God desires.

This is no small thing!

Isaiah 61:1-4 The Spirit of the Lord GOD *is* upon me; because the LORD hath anointed me to preach good tidings unto the meek; he hath sent me to bind up the brokenhearted, to proclaim liberty to the captives, and the opening of the prison to *them that are* bound; To proclaim the acceptable year of the LORD, and the day of vengeance of our God; to comfort all that mourn; To appoint unto them that mourn in Zion, to give unto them beauty for ashes, the oil of joy for mourning, the garment of praise for the spirit of heaviness; that they might be called trees of righteousness, the planting of the LORD, that he might be glorified. And they shall build the old wastes, they shall raise up the former desolations, and they shall repair the waste cities, the desolations of many generations.

Without the prompting of the Holy Spirit we don't think about restoring or about repairing "ruined cities." We don't think about repairing destinies. (There aren't many believers ministering in restoration.)

God wants me to raise up former desolations. Do you know what the old ruins and former desolations are?

Some of these examples concern churches and ministries or positions you have operated in before. These areas can be likened to "ruined cities" and "former desolations." God wants

# INCREASE OF REVELATION AND RESTORATION: REVEAL, RECOVER & RESTORE

to restore and repair these ruins and desolations. God wants to restore to the church the desolations of many generations.

I'm talking about past revivals that were cut short. Evangelism and healing ministries that ended with the death of the ministers Charles Finney, Smith Wigglesworth, Jack Coe, and A.A. Allan. Some of these ministries became desolate. Some of them had their reputations ruined by things that may not even be true. But God wants to restore their legacies.

This word is also to restore godly family heritages. Some of you need to apply this to your life in a personal way. You may have people in your family tree who loved the Lord, that were in the ministry even as prophets and evangelists. Believe and ask God for the spiritual destiny that your dad had, that your grandfather had (or whoever in your family line that the Holy Spirit brings to your attention). You have rights. They sowed, they labored and they died probably not yet receiving their promise, or seeing everything they thought God was going to allow them to see. You need to see it.

God wants to bless and bring restoration to the children and the children's children. Your blessing might go back three generations. You need to take it. There is an anointing to restore the desolations of many generations. What am I talking about? I am talking about restoring old wells. How is that going to happen?

You need to believe God and say: "My God, let their calling and ministry be restored in my generation." I believe that there is coming a generation that will receive the restoration of the desolations of many generations and that this will come in one last generation. Could it be us? Could we be that generation that receives much of what was lost in those former generations? Could we be that generation that digs up the wells of all those mighty men and women of God and all those great revivals? So let's look at several keys for changing what was to the reality of what God desires.

The devil came to steal and he has stolen from us, but God has provided a remedy. He's given us keys for walking in the ministry of restoration in order to reverse and restore those situations devastated by the enemy.

Here are three keys.

Christians are anointed to declare: "Restore!" No one says, "Restore!"

Isaiah 42:22 But this *is* a people robbed and spoiled; *they are* all of them snared in holes, and they are hid in prison houses: they are for a prey, and none delivereth; for a spoil, and none saith, Restore.

It's like God is saying,

"If somebody would have said, "Restore!" I would have delivered those people who were robbed. I would have taken them out of their prisons and the places that were plundered and I would have given them back sevenfold. If My children would have believed, they would have released jubilee anointing by "the rod of their mouth" just by speaking and proclaiming liberty for the captives. I need somebody to believe that I want to give the anointing for the ministry of restoration to repair people's lives and to rebuild what was ruined." (Jubilee is defined in Personal Breakthroughs.)

There is unction inside of us Holy Spirit words and decrees that when spoken out in authority, will break the power of the enemy. The decree might be over a marriage or finances. Simply declaring: "Restore!" is powerful. Things change. We

## INCREASE OF REVELATION AND RESTORATION: REVEAL, RECOVER & RESTORE

need to stand in the gap and believe that with one prophetic word spoken into the heavens, a breakthrough will come to raise up the foundations again. A breakthrough will bring the foundations back in a better way than was their former state. And then God will bless this with an increase; it might be a double portion or more!

Stand in faith and be "Repairers" and "Restorers" God calls us Repairers and Restorers. We need to restore people to their calling, their path, so that they can be planted and walk in it again. Prepare ourselves for the ministry of restoration. Remembering God's goodness is vital. David knew this.

Psalms 63:6, 7 When I remember thee upon my bed, *and* meditate on thee in the *night* watches. Because thou hast been my help, therefore in the shadow of thy wings will I rejoice.

Like David, we too, can lie on our bed and think about God's faithfulness to us. We can think about all the prophetic words that have come to us; about all the ways that God has used us; and about the healings we have seen and experienced in our own body. We can ponder all the instances where we saw God's hand of intervention. We can think about the gifts of the Holy Spirit and stir up those gifts and remember what God has promised us. He wants us to see ourselves walking in what He has promised us, dreaming again, and remembering God's faithfulness and the Father's love.

With our personal revelation about restoration, God's love, and His faithfulness, we are prepared to carry the anointing for restoration. Our personal breakthroughs will fuel our authority as ministers of restoration.

Throughout this Chapter we have discussed that God wants us to put our hope in Him. He will come as the Great

Restorer bringing the personal breakthroughs that we are crying out for. Still, I sense that some of you are burdened by fear, intimidation, and discouragement. It's like you are snared in a hole and you can't get out and you are in a prison and you can't get restored. But having said that, you need to remember that God wants to give you hope; renew your hope in Him. He wants you to have the victory!

Restoration can be likened to the year of Jubilee. In the context of Hebrew scriptures Jubilee was a year of rest; it was observed every 50th year by the Israelites. During this time certain slaves were set free, alienated property was restored to the former owners, and the soil rested, untilled. Freedom! God wants you to know that He will restore what has been plundered and robbed by the enemy. He wants you to taste freedom and restoration; to celebrate this in a "Jubilee way." Remember, what the Lord is about to restore, He is going to add blessings.

There's going to be increase and multiplication! Not only does He want to accomplish personal breakthroughs in your life and bring restoration to those devastated areas, He also wants to anoint you to minister restoration to others. It's the two-edged sword of restoration! No matter what place you are in spiritually today, whether it's a place of utter despair, a place of flickering hope, or a place of real trust and faith in God's ability to restore.

# INCREASE OF REVELATION AND RESTORATION: REVEAL, RECOVER & RESTORE

# About The Author

Bill Vincent is no stranger to understanding the power of God. Not only has he spent over twenty years as a Minister with a strong prophetic anointing, he is now also an Apostle and Author with Revival Waves of Glory Ministries in Litchfield, IL. Along with his wife, Tabitha, he, leads a team providing apostolic oversight in all aspects of ministry, including service, personal ministry and Godly character.

Bill offers a wide range of writings and teachings from deliverance, to experiencing presence of God and developing Apostolic cutting edge Church structure. Drawing on the power of the Holy Spirit through years of experience in Revival, Spiritual Sensitivity, and deliverance ministry, Bill now focuses mainly on pursuing the Presence of God and breaking the power of the devil off of people's lives.

His books 48 and counting has since helped many people to overcome the spirits and curses of Satan. For more information or to keep up with Bill's latest releases, please visit www.revivalwavesofgloryministries.com. To contact Bill, feel free to follow him on twitter @revivalwaves.

# Recommended Products

## By Bill Vincent

Overcoming Obstacles
Glory: Pursuing God's Presence
Defeating the Demonic Realm
Increasing Your Prophetic Gift
Increasing Your Anointing
Keys to Receiving Your Miracle
The Supernatural Realm
Waves of Revival
Increase of Revelation and Restoration
The Resurrection Power of God
Discerning Your Call of God
Apostolic Breakthrough
Glory: Increasing God's Presence
Love is Waiting – Don't Let Love Pass You By
The Healing Power of God
Glory: Expanding God's Presence
Receiving Personal Prophecy
Signs and Wonders
Signs and Wonders Revelations
Children Stories
The Rapture
The Secret Place of God's Power
Building a Prototype Church
Breakthrough of Spiritual Strongholds
Glory: Revival Presence of God
Overcoming the Power of Lust

Glory: Kingdom Presence of God
Transitioning Into a Prototype Church
The Stronghold of Jezebel
Healing After Divorce
A Closer Relationship With God
Cover Up and Save Yourself
Desperate for God's Presence
The War for Spiritual Battles
Spiritual Leadership
Global Warning
There Are Millions of Churches
Destroying the Jezebel Spirit
Awakening of Miracles
Deception and Consequences Revealed
Are You a Follower of Christ
Don't Let the Enemy Steal from You!
A Godly Shaking
The Unsearchable Riches of Christ
Heaven's Court System
Satan's Open Doors
Armed for Battle
The Wrestler
Spiritual Warfare: Complete Collection
Growing In the Prophetic
The Prototype Church: Complete Edition
Faith
The Rapture

# To Order:

## Email:
rwgcontact@yahoo.com

## Web Site:
www.revivalwavesofgloryministries.com[1]

1. http://www.revivalwavesofgloryministries.com

## Mail Order:

Revival Waves of Glory
PO Box 596
Litchfield, IL 62056

Shipping $5.00
If you mail an order and pay by check, make check out to Revival Waves of Glory.

# Don't miss out!

Visit the website below and you can sign up to receive emails whenever Bill Vincent publishes a new book. There's no charge and no obligation.

https://books2read.com/r/B-A-XHBC-WVVQB

**BOOKS 2 READ**

Connecting independent readers to independent writers.

# Also by Bill Vincent

Building a Prototype Church: Divine Strategies Released
Experience God's Love: By Revival Waves of Glory School of the Supernatural
Glory: Expanding God's Presence
Glory: Increasing God's Presence
Glory: Kingdom Presence of God
Glory: Pursuing God's Presence
Glory: Revival Presence of God
Rapture Revelations: Jesus Is Coming
The Prototype Church: Heaven's Strategies for Today's Church
The Secret Place of God's Power
Transitioning Into a Prototype Church: New Church Arising
Spiritual Warfare Made Simple
Aligning With God's Promises
A Closer Relationship With God
Armed for Battle: Spiritual Warfare Battle Commands
Breakthrough of Spiritual Strongholds
Desperate for God's Presence: Understanding Supernatural Atmospheres
Destroying the Jezebel Spirit: How to Overcome the Spirit Before It Destroys You!
Discerning Your Call of God

Glory: Expanding God's Presence: Discover How to Manifest God's Glory

Glory: Kingdom Presence Of God: Secrets to Becoming Ambassadors of Christ

Satan's Open Doors: Access Denied

Spiritual Warfare: The Complete Collection

The War for Spiritual Battles: Identify Satan's Strategies

Understanding Heaven's Court System: Explosive Life Changing Secrets

A Godly Shaking: Don't Create Waves

Faith: A Connection of God's Power

Global Warning: Prophetic Details Revealed

Overcoming Obstacles

Spiritual Leadership: Kingdom Foundation Principles

Glory: Revival Presence of God: Discover How to Release Revival Glory

Increasing Your Prophetic Gift: Developing a Pure Prophetic Flow

Millions of Churches: Why Is the World Going to Hell?

The Supernatural Realm: Discover Heaven's Secrets

The Unsearchable Riches of Christ: Chosen to be Sons of God

Deep Hunger: God Will Change Your Appetite Toward Him

Defeating the Demonic Realm

Glory: Increasing God's Presence: Discover New Waves of God's Glory

Growing In the Prophetic: Developing a Prophetic Voice

Healing After Divorce: Grace, Mercy and Remarriage

Love is Waiting

Awakening of Miracles: Personal Testimonies of God's Healing Power

Deception and Consequences Revealed: You Shall Know the Truth and the Truth Shall Set You Free

Overcoming the Power of Lust

Are You a Follower of Christ: Discover True Salvation

Cover Up and Save Yourself: Revealing Sexy is Not Sexy

Heaven's Court System: Bringing Justice for All

The Angry Fighter's Story: Harness the Fire Within

The Wrestler: The Pursuit of a Dream

Beginning the Courts of Heaven: Understanding the Basics

Breaking Curses: Legal Rights in the Courts of Heaven

Writing and Publishing a Book: Secrets of a Christian Author

How to Write a Book: Step by Step Guide

The Anointing: Fresh Oil of God's Presence

Spiritual Leadership: Kingdom Foundation Principles Second Edition

The Courts of Heaven: How to Present Your Case

The Jezebel Spirit: Tactics of Jezebel's Control

Heaven's Angels: The Nature and Ranking of Angels

Don't Know What to Do?: Discover Promotion in the Wilderness

Word of the Lord: Prophetic Word for 2020

The Coronavirus Prophecy

Increase Your Anointing: Discover the Supernatural

Apostolic Breakthrough: Birthing God's Purposes

The Healing Power of God: Releasing the Power of the Holy Spirit

The Secret Place of God's Power: Revelations of God's Word

The Rapture: Details of the Second Coming of Christ

Increase of Revelation and Restoration: Reveal, Recover & Restore

Restoration of the Soul: The Presence of God Changes Everything

Building a Prototype Church: The Church is in a Season of Profound of Change

Keys to Receiving Your Miracle: Miracles Happen Today

The Resurrection Power of God: Great Exploits of God

Transitioning to the Prototype Church: The Church is in a Season of Profound of Transition

Waves of Revival: Expect the Unexpected

The Stronghold of Jezebel: A True Story of a Man's Journey

Glory: Pursuing God's Presence: Revealing Secrets

Like a Mighty Rushing Wind

Steps to Revival

Supernatural Power

The Goodness of God

The Secret to Spiritual Strength

The Glorious Church's Birth: Understanding God's Plan For Our Lives

God's Presence Has a Profound Impact On Us

Spiritual Battles of the Mind: When All Hell Breaks Loose, Heaven Sends Help

A Godly Shaking Coming to the Church: Churches are Being Rerouted

Relationship with God in a New Way

The Spirit of God's Anointing: Using the Holy Spirit's Power in You

The Magnificent Church: God's Power Is Being Manifested

Miracles Are Awakened: Today is a Day of Miracles

Prepared to Fight: The Battle of Deliverance

The Journey of a Faithful: Adhering to the teachings of Jesus Christ

Ascension to the Top of Spiritual Mountains: Putting an End to Pain Cycles

After Divorce Recovery: When I Think of Grace, I Think of Mercy and Remarriage

A Greater Sense of God's Presence: Learn How to Make God's Glory Visible

Do Not Allow the Enemy to Steal: To a Crown of Righteousness, a Crown of Thorns

There Are Countless Churches: What is the Cause of Global Doom?

Creating a Model Church: The Church is Undergoing Considerable Upheaval

Developing Your Prophetic Ability: Creating a Flow of Pure Prophetic Intent

Christ's Limitless Riches Are Unsearchable: God Has Chosen Us to Be His Sons

Faith is a Link Between God's Might and Ours

Increasing the Presence of God: The Revival of the End-Times Is Approaching

Getting a Prophecy for Yourself: Unlocking Your Prophecies with Prophetic Keys

Getting Rid of the Jezebel Spirit: Before the Spirit Destroys You, Here's How to Overcome It!

Getting to Know Heaven's Court System: Secrets That Will Change Your Life

God's Resurrected Presence: Revival Glory is Being Released

God's Presence In His Kingdom: Secrets to Becoming Christ's Ambassadors

God's Healing Ability: The Holy Spirit's Power is Being Released

God's Power of Resurrection: God's Great Exploits

Heaven's Supreme Court: Providing Equal Justice for All
Increasing God's Presence in Our Lives: God's Glory Has Reached New Heights
Jezebel's Stronghold: This is the Story of an Actual Man's Journey
Making the Shift to the Model Church: The Church Is In the Midst of a Major Shift
Overcoming Lust's Influence: The Way to Victory
Pursuing God's Presence: Disclosing Information
The Plan to Take Over America: Restoring, We the People and the Power of God
Revelation and Restoration Are Increasing: The Process That Reveals, Recovers, and Restores
Burn In the Presence of the Lord
Revival Tidal Waves: Be Prepared for the Unexpected
Taking down the Demonic Realm: Curses and Revelations of Demonic Spirits
The Apocalypse: Details about Christ's Second Coming
The Hidden Resource of God's Power
The Open Doors of Satan: Access is Restricted
The Secrets to Getting Your Miracle
The Truth About Deception and Its Consequences
The Universal World: Discover the Mysteries of Heaven
Warning to the World: Details of Prophecies Have Been Revealed
Wonders and Significance: God's Glory in New Waves
Word of the Lord
Why Is There No Lasting Revival: It's Time For the Next Move of God
A Double New Beginning: A Prophetic Word, the Best Is Yet to Come

Your Most Productive Season Ever: The Anointing to Get Things Done

Break Free From Prison: No More Bondage for the Saints

Breaking Strongholds: Taking Steps to Freedom

Carrying the Glory of God: Igniting the End Time Revival

Breakthrough Over the Enemies Attack on Resources: An Angel Called Breakthrough

Days of Breakthrough: Your Time is Now

Empowered For the Unprecedented: Extraordinary Days Ahead

The Ultimate Guide to Self-Publishing: How to Write, Publish, and Promote Your Book for Free

The Art of Writing: A Comprehensive Guide to Crafting Your Masterpiece

The Non-Fiction Writer's Guide: Mastering Engaging Narratives

Spiritual Leadership (Large Print Edition): Kingdom Foundation Principles

Desperate for God's Presence (Large Print Edition): Understanding Supernatural Atmospheres

From Writer to Marketer: How to Successfully Promote Your Self-Published Book

Unleashing Your Inner Author: A Step-by-Step Guide to Crafting Your Own Bestseller

Becoming a YouTube Sensation: A Guide to Success

The Art of Content Creation: Tips and Tricks for YouTube

Signs and Wonders Revelations: Experience Heaven on Earth

Watch for more at
https://revivalwavesofgloryministries.com/.

# About the Author

Bill Vincent is no stranger to understanding the power of God. Not only has he spent over twenty years as a Minister with a strong prophetic anointing, he is now also an Apostle and Author with Revival Waves of Glory Ministries in Litchfield, IL. Along with his wife, Tabitha, he, leads a team providing apostolic oversight in all aspects of ministry, including service, personal ministry and Godly character.

Bill offers a wide range of writings and teachings from deliverance, to experiencing presence of God and developing Apostolic cutting edge Church structure. Drawing on the power of the Holy Spirit through years of experience in Revival, Spiritual Sensitivity, and deliverance ministry, Bill now focuses mainly on pursuing the Presence of God and breaking the power of the devil off of people's lives.

His books 50 and counting has since helped many people to overcome the spirits and curses of Satan. For more information or to keep up with Bill's latest releases, please visit www.revivalwavesofgloryministries.com. To contact Bill, feel free to follow him on twitter @revivalwaves.

Read more at https://revivalwavesofgloryministries.com/.

# About the Publisher

Accepting manuscripts in the most categories. We love to help people get their words available to the world.

Revival Waves of Glory focus is to provide more options to be published. We do traditional paperbacks, hardcovers, audio books and ebooks all over the world. A traditional royalty-based publisher that offers self-publishing options, Revival Waves provides a very author friendly and transparent publishing process, with President Bill Vincent involved in the full process of your book. Send us your manuscript and we will contact you as soon as possible.

Contact: Bill Vincent at rwgpublishing@yahoo.com

CPSIA information can be obtained
at www.ICGtesting.com
Printed in the USA
LVHW041131240523
747873LV00001B/185